Contents

Foreword

When Georges Izmidlian mentioned to me that he was going to write this book, I suggested that he should call it 'The Plain Man's Guide to Oriental Carpets and Rugs'. After reading his first manuscript, I offered him an alternative title, 'How to Invest Money and Enjoy It'.

Georges' outlook, however, is always factual and meticulous – and so he rejected both my title suggestions. He felt it to be his duty to avoid doubt or misrepresentation, and being such a stickler for truth, as was his late father, he stuck to his title, which he maintains does indeed mean what it says.

As a carpet merchant himself, little has infuriated him more than to see, increasingly, reproductions – albeit often handmade – being passed off as if of equal value to a 'real' oriental.

Apart from the beauty and craftsmanship which is inherent in a handmade rug, the origin of the piece is often the hallmark of value and so this element of origin can be the major factor when looked at from the point of view of investment and resale.

To avoid encroaching further on my colleague's pitch, I would underline the advice which he has given throughout this book to the first-time buyer whose knowledge is limited; buy your rug from a reputable establishment – avoid itinerant salesmen and auctions – there are no bargains for the non-specialist.

The recent interest shown in Islamic art has given a tremendous impetus to the sale of real oriental carpets and rugs and in this book the author has been able to pass on to the reader a very lucid and readable exposition of an ancient craft which has survived to this day in its original form.

With the steady march towards mechanised mass production and the special emphasis on industrialisation which increasingly motivates the carpet producing nations, it is very doubtful whether this craft, which is predominantly an individual and personal effort, will be able to survive – at any rate in its present dimension.

So I do hope that the reader will, with the aid of this admirable book, purchase before it is too late a beautiful rug to enjoy in his lifetime, and pass on as an heirloom to his children.

David Futerman
Chairman
P & O Carpets Ltd
London W1

Oriental Rugs and Carpets Today

How to Choose and Enjoy Them

With 34 plates in full colour,
16 in black and white, 50 drawings

Georges Izmidlian

HIPPOCRENE
BOOKS, INC.

New York, N.Y.

To my late father
Petrak Izmidlian
who introduced me to the world of oriental carpets

I must acknowledge the help received from George Speaight and my wife Beryl, without whose assistance and encouragement this book would never have been published.

The colour plates are reproduced from photographs of rugs in the possession of P & O Carpets Ltd, 5a Aldford Street, London W1, with the exception of Plates 1, 8, 11, 15, 20, 35, 39 and 42 from the collection of Mrs G. Izmidlian and Plates 17 and 37 from the collection of Mrs L. D. Futerman. Plate 34 was photographed by the author. The excellent line drawings are by Denys Baker.

© Georges Izmidlian 1977
© Georges Izmidlian 1983

ALL RIGHTS RESERVED

HIPPOCRENE BOOKS, INC.
171 Madison Avenue
New York, N.Y. 10016

Library of Congress Cataloging in Publication Data
Izmidlian, Georges.
    Oriental rugs and carpets today.
    1. Rugs, Oriental. 1. Title.

ISBN 0-88254-801-8 (Hardback)

ISBN 0-88254-800-X (Paperback)

Printed in Great Britain

Author's Note

Many excellent books have been published in recent years on oriental rugs and carpets, but most of these have concentrated their attention upon very fine and antique pieces, and have perhaps given the impression that oriental carpets are works of art only to be gazed at upon the walls of museums. There is a very real need, in my opinion, for a book that deals primarily with what is being made today, and which will help any one thinking of buying a carpet to choose with knowledge and discrimination. The traditional art of hand-knotting real oriental carpets is still alive today in the countries of the Middle East; and it is still possible to furnish your home with examples of these wonderful objects of craftsmanship. It is hoped that this book will not only help the reader to appreciate oriental carpets of the past but will inspire him actually to want to possess at least one for himself. Many of the pieces illustrated may be seen, handled and examined, without prior arrangement, at my West End premises.

Georges Izmidlian

Note to Second Edition

This edition (1983) has been completely revised in the light of developments since 1977.

Note: The size of a piece is the length and breadth of the piled area, taken through the centre. Metric sizes in the text are approximate conversions.

1 The Nomad Rug

From time immemorial nomad tribes have travelled, with their flocks, across the high plateaux of Central Asia. Abraham was the leader of such a tribe perhaps two thousand years before Christ; and even today some nomad or semi-nomad tribes still make their way in search of fresh pastures across the bare uplands of Iran, Afghanistan, Transcaucasia and Turkey.

The ground across which they journey is brown and arid; the only vegetation might be some thinly scattered thorny jujubee or gnarled, stunted oaks; the only wild life they might encounter would be coveys of red-legged buff partridge or a flock of swooping blue bee-eaters; the heat is like a furnace in summer, the cold is bitter on winter nights. The nomads travel through this semi-desert, sustained by the milk and flesh of their vast herds of sheep and goats. They hug the streams which provide drinking water for their herds until they reach new grass under the freshly-melted snow on a summer pasturage or shelter in a lowland valley during the winter months.

Every night during their trek, and for months on end when they settle, they will sleep in black tents of goatskin, perhaps eight paces long by five paces wide, supported by four poles. Here, after a hard day's toil on the barren hills, they will seek for rest and comfort; even for a brief foretaste of the Islamic paradise. And here, over the centuries, there has developed an astounding flowering of technique and art, for the interiors of these black tents were hung with multi-coloured woven cloths and the hard ground was made soft with cushions and rugs.

For the making of these cloths and rugs there was nothing but the materials with which they journeyed. The wool of the hardy sheep was sheared, washed in a stream, carded with long-toothed combs, and then spun into thread with a simple spindle. (It is easy enough to twist a few feet of thread from a handful of sheep's wool with the help of a weighted stick, but thousands of feet would be needed for even one small rug; and nomad tribeswomen did not usually possess even the mechanism of a spinning wheel.)

The wool thus produced was the grey or brown of the sheep's coat. It could be used in its natural colour, or it could be dyed. For dyes the nomads made use of the vegetable sources around them. The root of the madder plant yields a red dye; the flowers and leaves of the reseda plant or the saffron crocus give yellow, as do vine leaves, or pomegranate skins, or a certain fungus; the indigo plant gives blue; ripe turmeric berries give green; walnut shells or oak bark give shades of brown; oak apples produce black. Some colours came from animal sources: sheep's blood, or a swarm of coccus dried and crushed, or the shells of a louse that lives on the kermes oak, produce a red colour. The wool was always treated with sheep's dung before immersion in the dyeing vat, its albumen rendering the dyes more brilliant and longer lasting.

Then, armed with great hanks of softly dyed wool, came the weaving. The nomad loom is extremely simple, consisting of two oak branches – as straight as can be found – an arm's length wide, pegged six or eight feet apart on the ground. Tightly stretched from one beam to the other, and closely set together, are the lengthwise threads, the warp of the material. Starting from the bottom, the weaver then threads another network of threads from side to side, in and out of the warp, to make up the weft. In its simplest form this produces a length of woollen cloth, its thickness depending upon the thickness of the thread with which it is woven and on the tightness of the weaving. Sufficiently thick, or multi-plied, thread will produce a cloth substantial enough to put on the floor as a rug.

Patterns can be introduced into fabrics woven in this way. In between the weft threads that hold the material together, pieces of different-coloured thread can be woven in various lengths to form designs upon the body of the material. This produces a kind of smooth rug, without any pile, known as kilim.

The next step towards the creation of the true carpet came when the weavers started twisting short lengths of wool round the warp threads and in between each row of weft. These tufts of wool produced a warm, soft pile. Every kind of pattern – stylized renderings of flowers, birds and animals, or just geometrical shapes – was made possible by choosing tufts of different-coloured wool.

Nomad tribes do not fit easily into the structure of a modern state, which expects its citizens to attend schools, fill up census forms, perform military service, and pay taxes; only a few such tribes survive today. But the technique and artistry of their rugs and carpets have provided the foundation upon which the tradition of the oriental carpet has been based. The best oriental carpets retain the basic simplicity, the natural sense of colour values, the instinctive feeling for design, and the pride in good craftsmanship – even the slight irregularities which are the hallmark of an individual work of art – of the original nomad rug.

7

2 The Development of Oriental Carpets

As the manufacture of rugs and carpets was extended from nomads to village communities and then to workshops in towns, the techniques became more varied and more sophisticated.

The range of basic materials was extended from sheeps' wool to include cotton and silk, as well as goats' hair and camel hair. Wool is in many ways an excellent material for carpets but it tends not to lie quite flat on the floor, and may become distorted with use. It has been found in practice that a foundation of strong undyed cotton for warp and weft provides a firm structure for the wool pile to be knotted into; it shrinks evenly if washed and does not buckle. Silk can be used for the warp, providing a fine and un-stretchable foundation for a good-quality carpet; when used for the knots it produces a very effective sheen but the resulting pile lacks elasticity and the carpet will not stand up to hard wear. Goat and camel hair have been used effectively in certain areas, but supplies are not large enough for them to make any effective contribution to carpet making today.

The scarcity of natural materials and the enormous labour involved in converting them into dyes created great problems in the dyeing of the yarn needed for carpet manufacture. When aniline dyes, produced from chemical substances, were first introduced at the end of the nineteenth century they were welcomed by the lazier carpetmakers of the Middle East; but it was found that the colours produced were harsh, and some faded rapidly and some not at all; the whole reputation of oriental carpets was endangered. In 1903 the Persian government stopped the import of aniline dyes and forbade their use in carpet manufacture; this ban was not lifted until after World War I. Since that date it is fair to say that the quality of synthetic dyes has improved enormously; almost all carpets made today are woven from synthetically dyed yarn. The results are, however, pleasing only so far as the manufacturers have succeeded in reproducing – as they are now doing – the soft natural shades of the vegetable dyes that the nomads first coaxed from the barren earth thousands of years ago.

The looms have developed in detail but not in principle. The horizontal loom, laid on the ground and with only top and bottom beams, could be unstaked and rolled up with the partly completed rug on it, and carried on the back of a horse, camel or donkey, whenever the tribe moved on. A development of this was the rigid vertical cottage loom, which was supported by two side beams and was placed upright. Its width could still not easily extend further than the reach of one person sitting before it, so that carpets made on such looms must always be narrow. But they could be made as long as was wanted, as the warp threads were not tied to the top bar, as in the nomad loom, but were wound round it and then round the bottom bar. The completed carpet was wound on to a roller at the bottom of the frame. In this way the working area could be adjusted so that it was always at a suitable height for the weaver sitting or squatting before it. In both nomad and cottage looms an additional bar is needed as a 'shed' to separate every alternate strand of the warp, so that the weft thread can be passed smoothly through from one side to the other, binding the whole tightly together.

Carpet factories have been established for many years now in towns, though their methods are still based on hand manufacture and they bear no resemblance to factories as Europeans or Americans understand them. In these workshops large looms can be installed, so that carpets of considerable width can be made. The weavers often sit side by side on planks, which are pulled up as the work advances so as to avoid resetting the material too frequently.

Such procedures would be applicable to the weaving of any kind of material, or of a smooth kilim rug, but it is, of course, the tying of the knots that creates the tufted pile which is the essence of a carpet. These knots can only be tied by hand – no machine can duplicate hand-knotting – and the quality of a carpet depends to a large extent upon their closeness. Strictly speaking they are not true knots, as the lengths of yarn are twisted, rather than knotted, round the strands of the warp.

Turkish knot

Persian knot

There are two main types of knot used in oriental carpets. The Turkish, or Giordes, knot is made by twisting the length of yarn so that both ends of it come up between two strands of warp; there will then be two strands with no tufts between them, then two strands with two tufts, and so on. The Persian, or Senneh knot, is twisted so that a tuft appears between each strand of warp; this results in a far finer appearance, as one warp ends up almost on

9

top of the other instead of side by side as with the Giordes knot.

In practice there is really little difference between the results obtained by the two methods of knotting. The names are in any case not entirely accurate, as the Turkish knot is used in some parts of Persia, and the Persian knot in some parts of Turkey as well as in India and China. But broadly speaking the Turkish knot probably originated in the Near East and the Persian knot in the Far East. It is not easy to tell at a glance which kind of knot has been used on a carpet, but careful examination will usually reveal the method. If you examine the back, the Turkish knot shows two 'bumps' for each coloured knot, the Persian only one; best of all, if you have a piece cut off a carpet you can unpick it from the back and learn a great deal about carpet making in this way. Most good carpet merchants have damaged fragments and some will give you a piece to unpick at home.

It is difficult for westernised men and women, brought up in the machine age, to realise that the soft pile of the carpets on which they walk so un-thinkingly has been created by this laborious process of twisting hundreds of thousands of tiny knots. The work is so delicate that it is usually done by young women and children, who become extremely quick at it; an average weaver will tie up to 1,000 knots an hour, each knot taking only three or four seconds. She may well tie 10,000 knots in a day. Some workers will tie even more. But a good carpet may have over 100 knots to every square inch; a finely knotted carpet over 300; some carpets are known with over 2,000; others with no more than 10. So a quality rug measuring 8ft × 5ft may require a million separate knots; this might take one weaver a 100 days, or four months, to complete. And how much does the European or American buyer pay for it?

There are ways of reducing the number of knots – by tying them round three or four warp threads, for instance, instead of two, or by increasing the thickness or number of the weft threads between each row of knots. The result will still be a genuine handmade oriental carpet, but one of lesser quality and naturally of lower price. Only a well-informed and specialist dealer can point out these differences, which will become apparent to the layman only over years of use, when the carpet wears out more quickly than one would have hoped. This is particularly prevalent with open ground Kirmans.

It is difficult to see whether more or thicker weft threads have been used, but it is possible easily to find out whether the jufti knot (round three or more warps) has been used. This will be found most frequently in the plain ground of carpets, mainly Kirmans, where, because there is no design, the smaller number of knots will not be readily apparent. To check this, fold the carpet over and with one hand feel the double thickness of the border and with the other the double thickness of the ground. If the latter feels thinner it will wear more quickly than the patterned area and even if it is cheaper than a carpet that has been properly made it would be better to shun it.

In between each row of knots there will come one or more rows of weft.

When these have been threaded through, the whole line of weft and knots will be bound tightly together by being pulled down by a kind of iron comb that is drawn down through the warp threads. The result is so firm that it is impossible to pull the knots out from the front of the carpet. The only way to remove a knot is to unpick it from the back, and even that is not easy.

The yarn used for tying the knots is drawn from a skein, wound round two warps, and then roughly trimmed by the weaver with a knife, which often has a hook on the end that is used to help in knotting. This leaves a shaggy pile about three-quarters of an inch (2cm) long.

When, at last, the required length of carpet has been completed it will be taken or cut off the loom. The loose ends of warp are then often left just as they are, but sometimes the warps both at the top and bottom will be tied together in groups to form a fringe which may be long or short. Then corded selvedge will be sewn down each side.

Finally the pile of the carpet – that is, the length of the tufts after the knots have been tied – will be trimmed to a uniform thickness by a specialist work-man with a pair of curved shears. A deep pile does not necessarily indicate a superior quality carpet; a short pile shows up the pattern better, and indeed there is a Persian saying, 'The thinner the carpet, the richer the Persian'.

The finished carpet is then washed. This process, in which certain chemicals are added to the water, brings out the colours and imparts a lustrous sheen to the whole. The carpet is now ready for sale.

Several travellers have described the scene in a modern carpet workshop in the Middle East, with looms perhaps 12ft high × 20ft wide and rows of children squatting on boards, like scaffolding, as their nimble fingers fly in and out tying the knots of the carpet. Each child would have a pattern pinned before him to show what colour yarn to use for each knot, or the overseer might chant out the colours. It may seem a hard and laborious life for little children – and under Iranian law children under twelve years of age may now not be employed in such factories – but we are told that they joked and sang as they worked, chanting work songs directed to the other children whose task was to see that supplies of the requisite coloured skeins of wool were always hanging within their reach. The workshop would ring with their voices chanting 'Pass us the red, the pretty pretty red, pass us the red, oh the red' as the patterns formed upon the looms.

3 Design

When the nomads began to introduce designs into their rugs, they turned for inspiration to the natural objects that surrounded them – flowers, trees, animals, what they could see in the sky, and the objects furnishing their tents. The pattern of a woven carpet, however, is basically composed of straight lines ruled parallel to its shorter two sides, and the process of adapting any image to this technique of depiction inevitably involved considerable simplification. In the course of time these simplified shapes became more and more stylized into what may seem merely abstract patterns. Careful study will, however, often reveal these natural objects in the pattern of an oriental carpet today, for the basic designs of the nomads are still used.

Among shapes inspired by flowers or trees we find *palmettes*, which are large flowers seen as if in section; *rosettes*, any arrangements of flower petals arranged symmetrically around a central calyx; leaves, often a palm leaf leaning sideways in a highly stylized form called a *boteh;* and tendrils, which are often combined to form an *arabesque*. Animals depicted include birds, butterflies, peacocks, dragons, hounds, horses, camels and leopards. The sky inspired stars and a thin wavy device known as a *cloudband* which originated in China. Household objects include vases, lamps and candlesticks.

The Islamic religion, especially in the Sunnite form, forbade any depiction of living creatures; and this encouraged not only the stylization of the shapes already described but the development of purely abstract patterns composed of geometrical shapes. Important among these are the *gul*, which is basically a polygon, usually eight-sided, with more or less elaboration; the *swastika*, the use of which can be traced as far back as 6000 BC; and increasingly rarely the badge of *Tamerlane*, a triangular arrangement of three balls. A number of these shapes will often be grouped within a medallion or cartouche as the centrepiece of a carpet design.

The pattern of a carpet is usually arranged in a central field, surrounded by a border. The central field will often have one or more large motifs in the middle, with smaller motifs filling the corners. The border will, in fact, usually consist of one or more narrow borders round the outside edge of the carpet, a broader border, and then one or more narrower borders enclosing the central field.

A distinctive type of carpet is one carrying the Hunting design (Plate 13). These were introduced about the middle of the sixteenth century and depicted huntsmen, often on horseback, pursuing various species of wild animals. We can see, for example, leopards, antelopes, lions and wolves, all quite naturalistically depicted. The background is usually filled with twining tendrils of branches or leaves. An interesting feature is the complete absence of perspective. A mountain is often as high as a tree, which is smaller than a horse but the same size as a plant. There may be a large cartouche in the centre of the field and the wide border was often very beautifully decorated. These carpets closely reflect the designs of contemporary Persian miniature paintings.

Somewhat similar are the Garden design carpets (Plates 2 and 20), which originated at about the same time, under the influence of the Persian court, but reached their peak of popularity in the eighteenth and early nineteenth century. In these carpets the field depicted the layout of a garden, with flower-beds, winding paths, pools and streams; birds were often shown on the branches of the trees and fish swimming in the water. Carpets with this design are still made, but it now takes a much simpler and more stylized form.

An easily recognisable design is the Hatchli (Plate 44). This consists of a broad cross dividing the field of the rug into four compartments. It was often used on the rugs that hung over the entrances to tents. It had no Christian significance, and is found on rugs from all over Central Asia; the ornamented patterns between the arms of the cross are supposed to symbolize the nomad's dream of looking out from the beams of a proper doorway to flowering fields.

A carpet of a quite special design is the prayer rug (Plates 26, 43 and 50). This can be readily recognised as it is not symmetrical but depicts a pointed arch, or *mehrab*, at one end of the central field. This motif was copied from the architecture of mosques and these carpets were originally intended for prayer. The rug was placed with the mehrab pointing towards Mecca, and a small amount of holy earth from Mecca might be placed on the spandrel of the arch, so that the worshipper, kneeling on the rug, might touch the sacred earth with his forehead as he prostrated himself. The mehrab is sometimes flanked by two pillars of Wisdom and a lamp is suspended from the arch.

The date is sometimes knotted into a rug (Plates 24 and 25), and it would be helpful for the student of carpets to learn the form in which the arabic numerals appear in arabic script, which is not identical with the forms they take in conjunction with the roman alphabet. The dates, however, are usually not those of the Christian calendar but of the Islamic Hegira calendar; to convert into the Christian calendar one must divide by 33, subtract the quotient from the Islamic date, and add 622. Thus the Islamic date 1353 represents the year AD 1934:

$$1353 \div 33 = 41$$
$$1353 - 41 = 1312$$
$$1312 + 622 = 1934$$

0	1	2	3	4	5	6	7	8	9

13

Carpets woven by Armenian Christians, however, may show dates according to the Christian calendar. Inscriptions in Kufic or other arabic script are also sometimes introduced into the design of a carpet; these may be texts from the Koran, or personal messages from the weaver or the patron, or the weaver's signature – usually in the top border. Rugs woven by Armenians frequently carry inscriptions in Armenian script, which is quite different from all forms of arabic.

Various types of pattern have been given distinctive names. For instance, a central field filled with elaborate palmettes inspired by the lily is called the Shah Abbas pattern, after a famous Persian ruler in whose reign the pattern was popular and who was the father of the Persian renaissance in his capital, then Ispahan. The leaf pattern called Miriboteh, Serabend or Pine Cone, consisting of identical motifs scattered over the field, was the inspiration of the design of Paisley shawls. A diamond central shape flanked by four curled leaves is called the Herati or Feraghan pattern. Many other different names are applied to various combinations of patterns; as one's knowledge of oriental carpets grows one can delight in recognising these, but too many strange names are confusing to the newcomer and it is unnecessary to learn them all in order to appreciate the beauty of oriental carpets.

The naturalistic portraits and illustrations that have been introduced in recent centuries (Plate 11) make a distinctive type of carpet design. During the nineteenth century the technique of knotting became so sophisticated that portraits of almost photographic realism were introduced into carpets, and these are sometimes still made, often to special order. During World War II, at a time when German influence was powerful in Iran, a carpet factory in Tabriz made a large carpet carrying a portrait of Hitler. Today woodland landscapes, crowded with flora and fauna, or illustrations to the *Shah-Nameh* (Book of Kings) of Firdowsi are sometimes depicted on Persian carpets. Technically skilful though these are, the true carpet lover will almost certainly prefer designs based upon the traditional stylized patterns.

Attempts are sometimes made to find symbolic or esoteric meanings in the colour or patterns of oriental carpets, but these were almost certainly never in the minds of the original designers. There is a certain shade of green – the Prophet's Green – which is regarded as sacred by the Sunnite sect and so should not be trodden underfoot. This apart, the colours and patterns of an oriental carpet do not normally hold any obscure secret meaning. The oriental carpet is a supreme example of an object in which fine craftsmanship is combined with an instinctive feeling for what looks right. Though the nomad weavers and knotters had no education or art training, probably could neither read nor write, and made up their patterns as they worked, their results are works of art that have never been surpassed. Carpet factories today can do no better than follow the instinctive designs of their nomadic ancestors. Unfortunately they often follow old designs too closely and these pieces seem to lose their character and the apparent spontaneity of the original. Many look quite machine-made and the finest almost as though they were printed.

4 'Real' Carpets and their Countries of Origin

If you travel in Germany, where there has for long been a keen appreciation of and a great demand for oriental carpets, you will often see the term *echte Teppiche* – 'real carpets'. In Denmark it is *ægte Tæpper*, and so on elsewhere in Europe. What does this term 'real' mean?

In countries where an informed and discriminating body of opinion has grown up on the subject of oriental carpets, a distinction is drawn between those from Persia, Turkey, Afghanistan and Russia, and those from other areas which produce similar goods. Only the former are entitled to be described as 'real oriental carpets'. The latter, including carpets from Bulgaria, Romania, Yugoslavia, Greece, Hungary, Pakistan, India and China, are regarded as of less value.

What is the difference between 'real' carpets and the others? Both categories are hand-knotted floor coverings, made in the same way, often with very similar designs. The 'real' carpets do not necessarily have better wearing qualities; in fact other handmade carpets are often longer-lasting than a real carpet and, from this point of view, a better buy.

The reason for the distinction is that there is as yet no demand for used or secondhand carpets from the other areas, so they will tend to fall in value almost as fast as machine-made floor coverings like Wilton or Axminster. There is a good market for used and antique 'real' carpets, and these may be expected to hold and even increase their value with wear. The same principle holds good for old Indian and Chinese carpets and for early Axminsters, but in general it is safe to hold to the rule that, in the long run, it is best to buy a real oriental carpet. This point will be discussed in greater detail when we come to consider carpets as an investment.

In this book, therefore, we shall deal mainly with real oriental rugs and carpets, those from Persia, Turkey, Afghanistan and Russia.

Persia

Notwithstanding the discovery in Russia of the Pazyryk rug dated 300 BC, Persia is the original home of the real oriental carpet, and it is worth considering briefly how this came about. In about 500 BC the Persian empire stretched from the Indus in the east to the Aegean in the west; the control of this vast territory was seized by Alexander the Great for the Greeks, and then by the Parthian Arsacids and the native Sassanids, before the Muslim Arabs conquered the area in the seventh century AD. After a period of anarchy,

15

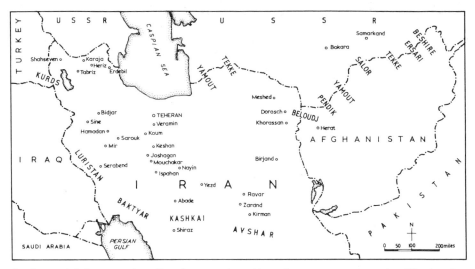

during which a native Persian nationalism began to assert itself, the first modern dynasty was established in the sixteenth century; a glorious period of art and literature followed, but in the nineteenth century Russia made considerable territorial gains on either side of the Caspian Sea. Revolutions in 1906 and 1927 lead to the collapse of the Qajar dynasty and the emergence of the modern state of Iran.

Throughout the greater part of this period the primitive life of the nomad tribes, already described, continued unchanged, but at the same time highly developed civilizations flourished in the chief towns. It was this conjunction of the traditional craft of carpet weaving with the emergence of conditions of wealth and luxury at the courts which led to the development of Persian carpets in their supreme artistic form. The same development can be seen in the superb tradition of Persian miniature painting, which reached its peak in the sixteenth century; these illuminated manuscripts, with their exquisite calligraphy and pure colours, depicting elegant figures, architecture and gardens, often include carpets in the house-furnishings illustrated. A passion for intricate detail, which nevertheless always remains within the broad sweep of the overall design, marks Persian art in all its forms – in its miniatures, in its calligraphy, in the patterned tiles of its architecture, and in its carpets.

Ever since western Europe began to appreciate the value of oriental carpets in the sixteenth century, the export of carpets has played an important part in the Persian economy. Modern Iran still takes great pride in its carpet tradition and the late Shah established royal factories where only the finest materials and methods of manufacture were employed, but today oil is of far greater importance than carpets in the economy of the state. With greatly increased oil revenues, Iran is a relatively rich country, even though some basic skills and materials are still scarce. Will the craft of knotting carpets by hand survive in the Iran of tomorrow? This generation of Persians may be the last to provide workers for the laborious task. And this generation of Europeans and Americans may be the last to be able to buy their exquisite products so comparatively cheaply.

Whatever changes the future may hold for Iran, Persian carpets will remain as evidence not only of the art and craftsmanship of the Persian people but as a sign of their gentle and civilized approach to life. Omar Khayyam is, in fact, better known in English-speaking countries, through Edward Fitzgerald's translation, than he is in Iran today, but he expressed a great truth about the Persian way of life when he wrote of taking his ease where 'still a Garden by the Water blows', of the Rose 'that never blows so red . . . as where some buried Caesar bled', of 'every Hyacinth the Garden wears', and of 'this delightful Herb whose tender Green Fledges the River's Lip on which we lean'. The Persian has always been a great lover of flowers. In his home he used to sit on the floor, not on chairs but on carpets. And some say that by introducing flowers into his carpets he feels he is still sitting in his garden, even indoors, and especially in winter. Many people do not realise just how cold it gets in Persia during the winter months, sometimes with up to three feet of snow.

Turkey

Turkey has had a carpet making tradition for as long as Persia. The first oriental carpets to be imported into western Europe were Turkish or, as they were then called, Anatolian. They were depicted in paintings by Holbein and Lotto in the early sixteenth century, the designs shown now being known by the names of these artists. The carpets are painted in a merchant's house or in similar settings; their purchase was clearly not limited to royalty or the very rich. One can also see that they were usually laid on tables rather than on the floor, a custom still common in Holland today.

For many centuries there was a thriving trade in Turkish carpets and in Persian carpets exported through Constantinople. The finest of Turkish manufacture were probably the Kum-Kapu and Hereke rugs, but even quite coarse carpets from Sivas, Sparta and Oushak were made of such excellent wool that they have outlasted many of the finest pieces produced elsewhere at the same time. The Anatolian carpets seldom portray men or animals in their designs, as the Sunnite Muslim sect, preponderant in Turkey, observes

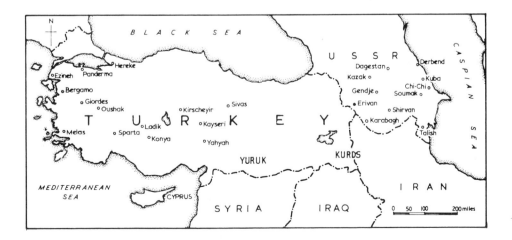

17

the Koran's injunction against the portrayal of living things more strictly than the Shiite sect, found in Persia.

In general, Turkish carpets are coarser than Persian ones but they give good wear. Large Turkish carpets were greatly favoured in Europe and America up to World War II, especially for libraries and dining-rooms, and many older readers will recall – and are probably still using – these carpets, with their almost invariable Oushak pattern in red and green with some blue. They were remarkably cheap; before the war a large carpet, 12ft × 9ft, could be bought for £22 15s. Their distinctive pattern was widely copied on cheap linoleum.

The better Turkish pieces were generally made by and largely for Armenians and Greeks, using imported Persian designs but always, of course, with the Turkish knot. Then in 1914, during a period of nationalist xenophobia, nearly two-thirds of the Armenian population was either deported or massacred, and in 1922, in similar circumstances, some two million Greek families were expelled from Turkey, though they had lived there for generations, and among them were most of the carpet weavers. The industry has never recovered from these losses, and in recent years production has been mostly of very poor quality.

Afghanistan

The early carpet traditions of Afghanistan were similar to those of Persia, but they have been maintained mainly by nomads and have been little affected – until recently – by the more sophisticated influences of the Persian court or by the taste of the European market. The carpets tend to be predominantly red in colour and the basic decoration consists of octagons – the Elephant's Footprint pattern as it is called; like those of Turkey, and for the same reasons, human and animal forms are almost never represented on Afghan carpets. Most of the nomad tribes in Afghanistan belong to the Turkomen racial group. The primitive vigour of their designs make their rugs among the best examples of nomad handicraft, and they take their place very effectively in the interior decoration of modern western homes.

Old Afghans, in which the colours have softened, are in particular demand today, and have become disproportionately expensive, mainly because only a small number have survived. They are still inexpensive, nevertheless, in comparison with Persians of similar age and quality. These old pieces would have been made some forty to sixty years ago and imported when they cost almost nothing; they were regarded then as the cheapest kind of rough carpeting and were often treated with little care in western homes. As is often the case, goods that were once cheap have practically disappeared while expensive goods have been carefully preserved. Country fairings which were treated as rubbish when they were bought are now scarce and expensive, while there is still plenty of fine old lace put away at the bottom of trunks; similarly old Afghan rugs are now scarcer than many fine carpets of the same age from other regions.

As in Persia, rugs from different Afghan villages show marked differences but these are not widely known or recognised outside the country. With a few exceptions, all rugs from Afghanistan are lumped together as Afghans and there is little of the fine distinction between different qualities that is such a feature of Persian, Turkish and Russian rug and carpet nomenclature.

The wool for Afghans is usually very good indeed and with wear becomes quite silky in texture. The warp and weft were always of wool, so these rugs should not be washed or wetted; recently production of cheaper types has been started with inferior wool for the knots and with cotton warp and weft, but it is said that export of these has been banned – perhaps only temporarily.

There is a vast production of rugs from Afghanistan, probably greater than for any other single quality (ie type). Most of them still come from nomad or village looms; there is some factory production, and the designs have the irregularity and little 'quirks' that distinguish the best handmade pieces. In the last few years some quite new designs have been developed locally and given the general name of Naksha-i-Gashta.

Afghan rugs and carpets are still relatively inexpensive, and offer some of the best value for money in the field of oriental carpets today.

Russia

This area at present comprises the Soviet republics of Georgia, Azerbaidjian, Armenia and Dagestan to the west of the Caspian Sea and, to the east, Turkmenistan. Until 1813 the area was governed from Persia, and throughout history it has been a meeting point for many of the races of the Middle East. Turkomen nomads have wandered over this territory for generations, producing rugs similar to those of their counterparts in Afghanistan; as recently as the 1930s an entire nomadic tribe, the Tekke Turkomans, migrated en masse across the border from Turkmenistan to settle in Iran. Persian and Turkish influences had little effect upon the carpets of the area, and in the remote and inaccessible valleys of the great mountain ranges old traditions were zealously preserved. The result has been that Caucasian carpets may represent an older tradition than is found in some Persian carpet centres today. Whatever the ultimate origins of their designs, Caucasian carpets – with a few exceptions – have certain features in common: the patterns are strongly geometrical, and even when human or animal figures are represented this is done by straight lines and severely angular shapes; there is none of the flowing tendril motifs or softly curving garden imagery of Persian carpets (except in carpets from the Karabagh region, where often the most floral of motifs are to be found, though their manufacture is usually attributed to Armenians). Today the old traditional nomad and village pattern of life is breaking down, but the USSR has attempted to preserve the technique of hand-knotted carpets and many carpets are being produced in state factories according to the traditional methods; there is, unfortunately, an inevitable loss of individual quality in the process of standardisation and most of the recent manufacture which is of poor wool, though using handmade techniques, looks very machine-made.

It must be said that modern Russian production from the USSR bears little resemblance to what most people mean when they refer to Caucasian rugs. The colours are the same, only not so fine; the stitch is the same, only coarser; the designs are the same, only simplified. Factory production simply cannot convey the character of individual handmade rugs.

Pakistan

Subsequent to the realignment of currencies in the seventies and eighties, there has been an enormous increase in the price of carpets from traditional sources – the homes of real carpets, particularly Persians. This, of course, has affected the whole trade but more so the cheaper end where poor and middle grade goods have become inordinately expensive whilst remaining very plentiful. Wholesalers have sought new and cheaper suppliers, and originally found them in an increased production from West Pakistan.

These carpets are made by Turkomen tribesmen now living in Pakistan and, of course, by the Pakistanis themselves. When production first started good wool was used, but then the quality deteriorated, though this has begun to improve due largely to Western influence. Kashmiri wool is generally used, though this is more suitable for clothing than a floor covering, so, whilst a new Pakistan carpet or rug looks most attractive and very silky, it is unlikely to last anywhere near as long as those from the older-established regions. The bulk of the production is in Bokara design, though now an increasing number are made with Persian, Turkish and even Afghan designs, as well as some of their own less attractive designs.

India

The carpet-making tradition in India goes right back to the time of the Moguls. The wool used is harder wearing than that used in Pakistan, and these carpets traditionally had a very long, rough pile. Because of the difficulty of obtaining a long enough fibre they had a great tendency to moult, and for years would shed hairs which would find their way into every corner. In the period after World War II and up to the early seventies, Indian weavers flooded the world with low-grade, off-white carpets and rugs, many of a wool and jute mixture. Chinese designs were frequently copied, and as cream or white was the usual colour they became dirty very quickly.

A few years ago the Indians started making cheap, poor copies of Persian Hamadans, but this was followed in the late seventies by the establishment of a completely new type of production. The combination of unemployment and low wages was harnessed under Western influence to start many new factories weaving shorter-pile carpets of Persian patterns, quite different from anything previously woven. They use good designs and colours and production has so increased that they are now called Indo-Persians. Carpets are already being woven based on Heriz, Gorovan, Mehraban, Shiraz, Mir, Abade and Wiesz designs, and doubtless other types will follow. Rugs are being produced of Shiraz, Abade, Kirman, Keshan, Koum and other designs, mostly on light grounds. As they are usually made of good wool they should be long-lasting floor coverings but cannot be regarded as investment items. At first, an attempt was made to copy the original knots so that the backs of each piece differed quite markedly, but now most look alike. The warps are generally of very thin, white twine, which helps to distinguish between an original Persian carpet and an Indo-Persian reproduction.

In Pakistan, and also India, production is more of an industry than a folk craft. Therefore, the designs are less inspirational and more likely to have been set by designers working in Western studios, though they are mostly based on traditional designs.

At the same time there has been a marked growth in the production of Kashmir rugs in north-west India; these must not be confused with Pakistan rugs made from Kashmir wool. Both are fine but Indian Kashmirs are made of harder, better wool and feel altogether more solid. At present, Indian production consists primarily of rugs of fine and very fine stitch, largely in Keshan, Kirman and other similar designs.

Other Countries

The Rumanians, and the Bulgarians which are slightly better quality, are both reasonably good carpets, sometimes finely made. They both copy old Persian designs almost exclusively, but these have usually been worked out so precisely that they are far too regular in appearance, and are therefore almost indistinguishable from a machine-made carpet. Because of their regularity they have neither the character nor the appeal of a real oriental, and whilst far more expensive than machine-made carpets they are only slightly less so than the real article. The Yugoslav carpets consist mainly of kilims.

Hungarian carpets are woven from thick wool in natural colours and introduce some attractive folk designs. In Greece many of the carpetmakers expelled from Turkey in 1922 set up their looms to continue their traditional handwork, and for a time the quality was equal to that of Turkish carpets; but in the course of time the Turkish tradition has tended to be lost and both the quantity and quality of oriental carpet manufacture in Greece has declined.

All the countries that we have considered so far share basically the same carpetmaking traditions. India and Pakistan in one direction, and the countries of eastern Europe in the other, have all drawn upon the great traditions of real oriental carpets from the Middle East. Whilst experts can distinguish between carpets from the different regions, their general style and appearance is broadly similar. With China we are clearly dealing with a different tradition altogether. The technique of weaving and knotting is the same, with general use of the Senneh knot, but silk rugs were produced in larger numbers than elsewhere, especially in Shantung which is famous for its natural silk industry. In their colours the Chinese carpetmakers have always preferred delicate shades of blue, yellow and rose, with much use of white; the strong reds and blues so often found in Persian carpets seldom appear. In their manufacture Chinese carpets are commonly left with a much deeper pile than is usual with Persian carpets. But it is their patterns that render Chinese carpets quite distinct.

The elements in the design of Chinese carpets are commonly the same as those found in other Chinese art, on porcelain, ivory, and paintings. Animals are often represented, chiefly the dragon but sometimes the phoenix, the elephant or the horse. Flowers are shown more naturalistically than on the carpets of the Middle East, and we find the lotus, the pomegranate, the peony, the daffodil and the peach blossom.

A distinct group of Chinese carpets are produced in Chinese Turkestan. Because of its geographical position in the extreme west of China, they have tended to be closer in style to the carpets of Persia or the Caucasus than to the main Chinese tradition. As these were always traded through Samarkand, they acquired this totally incorrect name. The quality of their weaving and knotting is poor, but they are in great demand on account of their beautiful designs and colours. They are often made from a very silky wool, which has poor wearing qualities. Many have faded or been bleached artificially so that much of the colour has been lost. All in all, they have become more suitable for decoration than for practical use but their soft pastel shades appeal to interior decorators.

A variant group from Kansu and Ningsia have rather greater Chinese characteristics and were probably marketed through Peking. Production was very small, but they proved particularly popular in the United States.

A particular feature of Chinese carpet patterns is the introduction of Buddhist and Taoist emblems which have symbolic associations. The main Buddhist symbols, for instance, are the conch that summons to prayer, the parasol that gives shade to healing herbs, the canopy that shields living creatures, the vase containing the water of perfect wisdom, the fish that symbolises salvation, the everlasting love knot, the lotus signifying purity, and the eight-spoked wheel symbolizing these eight symbols. These and many other symbols are sometimes repeated to form geometric patterns.

Chinese carpets enjoyed great popularity in Europe and the United States at the beginning of the twentieth century, especially for bedrooms, and a large export industry grew up. The manufacture of traditional carpets is well organised both in mainland China and in Hong Kong today; it is fair to say, however, that the deep luxurious pile of a Chinese carpet does not always cover a strong and firmly knotted foundation, though it is often very long-lasting. Recently the Chinese have started making rugs with Persian designs.

The Future

The future is hard to foresee, except that the production of handmade carpets will switch from high-cost countries to others where production is cheaper. This explains the transfer not only from Persia to India but also within Persia itself, where, for example, few looms are to be found today in Tabriz because of industrialization there, though it is reported that Tabriz carpets still continue to be made in the adjacent villages of Heriz and Ahar.

5 Names for Carpets and Rugs

Oriental pieces are not made in the exact measurements that are expected in Western factory-made goods; all one can do is to group carpets and rugs into certain named categories of size, which often relate to the ancient way of life of tent-dwelling peoples.

International usage normally applies the name carpet to any piece over 40 sq ft (4 sq m). Anything under this size is a rug. American usage, however, applies the term rug to *all* handmade carpets, and the term carpet to all machine-made carpets. In this book, we shall, in general, adopt the international usage for these terms.

Not quite classifiable either as rugs or carpets are Strips (Kenarés) and Kellays. Strips are, of course, long narrow pieces used for corridors and staircases. Their average width varies between 2ft 3in (70cm) and 3ft 9in (1·15m) and they can be of any length from 8ft (2·50m) to 30ft (9m). The longer a piece is the wider it tends to be.

Kellays are pieces generally about double the width but of the same length as a Strip. The word is of Persian origin and means a piece whose length is about double its width. Most Kellays measure about 10ft × 5ft (3·00 × 1·50m), 11ft × 5ft (3·30 × 1·50m) and 12ft × 6ft (3·60 × 1·50m), but the same name is applied also to pieces which measure up to 20ft (6m) long × 6ft (1·50m), 7ft (2m) or 8ft (2·50m) wide. In other words, it is frequently used as a term to describe any large piece other than a Strip, which is not of normal carpet or rug proportions.

Rugs are themselves divided into certain sub-groups according to size, but as units of measure tend to be elastic, and as most pieces were made originally for private use, they vary considerably in size even though they may have the same name.

Dozar is the name of the largest rug, which generally measures about 6ft 6in × 4ft 6in (2·00 × 1·40m) in width. The name comes from 'Do' being the Persian 'two', so a Dozar is a piece which measures about two zars in area, a Zar being about 12 to 16 sq ft (1 to 1·5 sq m) depending upon the region of production. A Sedjadé is of similar size.

A Zaronim, which means a zar and a half in Persian, is generally about 5ft 3in × 3ft 3in (1·60 × 1·00m) averaging about 18 to 20 sq ft (1·6 to 1·8 sq m).

Coming down in size, the next piece is known as a Namasé or Baby, which measures around 4ft × 2ft (1·20 × 0·60m), the average size being about 9 or

10 sq ft (0·80 or 0·90 sq m). A Baby is generally used as a bedside rug, or in front of fireplaces and French windows.

The next smaller size is a Mat (or Pushti), which measures about 4 or 5 sq ft (0·40 or 0·50 sq m). It is mainly used in doorways and when a door is closed against it, it acts as an excellent draughtproofer and a very attractive one at that. It is also used in front of a small piece of furniture or sometimes in front of a television set where a machine-made carpet underneath would get an excessive amount of wear.

Another, but now less common size, is the Mossul, which generally measures about 6ft 6in × 3ft 3in (2 × 1m). Many years ago this name was given to rugs which came from Mossul but today it is used to denote the size of rugs which come mainly from the Hamadan district.

Herek is another slightly unusual size, about 5ft × 2ft 3in (1·50 × 0·70m). This also is less common today and is also used as a bedside rug.

Apart from the above, which are all made to be used as floor-coverings, certain other items are woven and knotted in exactly the same way. Camel Bags are just like smallish rugs except that at one end the kilim is as big as the rug itself, so that when it is folded under it covers the whole of the back of the piece. The front (bag face) and back are then sewn together along the short sides, and this makes a large open-ended envelope or bag measuring about 5ft 3in (1·60m) wide. These are made to be used in pairs, one being lashed on each side of a camel.

The Saddle Bag, which is considerably smaller and which comes in 'pairs', is made with a bag at each end so that it hangs over a donkey's neck. Each bag measures about 2 or 3 sq ft (0·20 or 0·25 sq m). It is made like the Camel Bag with a length of piled rug, then an area of kilim of the same size, then sometimes a very small area of piled rug, then a similar area of kilim as before, and finally a further length of piled rug. The two ends are turned in and the sides sewn up. The piled area in the middle rests above the donkey's neck.

All these bags are used for carrying goods and personal belongings when travelling by horse, donkey or camel, but the larger Camel Bags are used for the carriage of merchandise and even of rocks and stones for road-making. Nomadic tribesmen, living primarily in tents, also stored clothes in them, so they can then be used as cushions or pillows, or even as a mattress for a small child on the floor of the tent.

In Western Europe, if the back is left on a Saddle Bag it can be stuffed with wool or feathers, or these days with some kind of foam-plastic, and used as a cushion; a Camel Bag, similarly stuffed, may be used as a large pouffe in front of the fire. If the backs of the bigger pieces are cut off and a fringe made on one side only, they can then be used as hearth or bedside rugs.

Pendjereliks are made in exactly the same way as any carpet or rug, but their size is very special. They generally measure between 4ft and 6ft (1·20 and 1·80m) wide and between 10in and 18in (25 and 45cm) in depth. After manufacture, a long woollen fringe between 2ft and 4ft (0·60 and 1·20m) in length is woven along the long side. A Pendjerelik is used in the Middle East over the entrances to tents and it acts rather like bead curtains in the Far East, keeping out the direct rays of the burning sun and some of the flies, but allowing in enough light and air for people to see what they are doing.

Pendjereliks are used in the West on the top of bookcases, in front of French windows or on windowsills as draught excluders.

Quite different from all the above is the kilim, which is woven in much the same way as any French tapestry but is quite smooth and is reversible; a few of them, however, known as Soumaks (which come mainly from Russia), have all the loose ends showing at the back rather like a piece of ordinary embroidery. Another type of kilim is the Jijim, which is also made by nomads, generally in very narrow bands between 6in and 12in (15 and 30cm) in width which are sewn together to make a large covering for a piece of furniture. If very fine, they are used like a shawl.

Many of these kilims have wonderful colours and the most primitive and interesting geometric designs; they are used in the West today in sun lounges or as picnic rugs outdoors. Many of the finest pieces are used as very hard, almost everlasting, upholstery fabric (as can be seen at Petworth House in Sussex).

Another unusual type of kilim is the Jolam. This is a tent band, widely used by the Turkomen and other nomadic tribes to decorate their yurts or tents. The Jolam measures anything from 2in to 2ft (5 to 60cm) in width and can be anything from 10ft to 100ft (3 to 30m) long. In recent years they have become very popular outside the Middle East for various purposes. The wider ones are sometimes used as rather impermanent stair carpets; their advantage over a normal oriental stair carpet is their enormous length in one piece, but obviously their wearing qualities cannot be compared with a normal piled runner. These of middle width are often used as pelmets. As these bands are not particularly expensive they are often cut up to make the face of cushions, to top stools, as table runners or on sideboards. When it was common for maids to be employed narrow lengths were used as bell pulls; very narrow ones can be used to decorate cushions. It is almost incredible that these beautiful strips of material are used by porters in the bazaars merely to secure their often heavy or cumbersome loads on their ever-bent backs.

Jolams are often very finely woven kilims, of excellent quality wool, but those most sought after are also heavily embroidered or with the pattern picked out in pile and are now very expensive. An interesting feature is that in a long Jolam the main design is contained in separate boxes about 2ft (60cm) long, each with a different and often fascinating motif.

6 Some Points to Look for

The Life of a Carpet

There are many reasons why oriental carpets have been renowned for centuries as the best floor-covering made by man. Primarily they bring so much warmth, light and cheerful colour into a room.

The best-known sound and heat insulator is still air, and the deep pile of an oriental carpet traps air between each fibre, like a thick woollen vest. On a sprung floor it provides sound insulation so that footsteps across the room do not echo. On a solid floor the oriental carpet provides heat insulation, protecting the feet from the cold ground underneath.

The pile is made of wool generally handspun from local sheep, which are usually miserable, rather scraggy beasts. These sheep live on poor and stony pastures, and over the centuries the various hardy breeds have developed a tough wiry wool which can withstand the abrasions of stones and coarse scrubland.

This wool is very springy and all real orientals show no footmarks, as the pile at once springs back into place. This is so important that many manufacturers of machine-made carpets are trying to compete by selling what they call non-crush pile. A pile which lacks this natural springiness will soon flatten until eventually it will look like patterned linoleum but far more unattractive. Putting down underlay is only a partial and temporary solution.

As the pile of an oriental carpet is so tough and springy it is the ends of the fibres which take the wear. If the pile flattens it is the side of the fibre that gets worn. As an example, if the thickness of a fibre is about 1/1000th of an inch and if the pile of a carpet is ¼ inch deep (ie 250/1000th of an inch), when it has had 1/1000th of an inch wear, a fibre which has flattened will be worn through its thickness, so the pile will soon measure only 1/6th inch deep. When it has had a little more wear it will be only 1/12th inch thick, whereas at this stage the pile of a good oriental carpet will be 248/1000th of an inch thick – a minute reduction on the original 250/1000th of an inch.

This is, of course, a somewhat theoretical example as in practice the pile of a carpet neither stands up completely vertical nor lies down completely flat; though as the pile gets worn it becomes more bristly and stands up straighter. What normally happens is that half the pile may be worn away in, say, twenty years; then half of what is left (that is, a quarter of the original) may go in the next fifteen or twenty years; and then half of what is then left will go in another fifteen or twenty years; and so on. It will take a very long time, or very intensive usage, to wear the pile of a good oriental carpet right away. When this happens it usually takes the form of a bald patch by a doorway, and we shall suggest in Chapter 8 how this may be avoided.

It can therefore be readily seen how important it is to buy a carpet where the wool stands up not only when the piece is bought but also throughout its life. It is not the length of the wool that matters but whether the pile is so tight and vertical, even if very short, that it will not lie down. This gives oriental carpets such a long life that it is not unusual to see pieces which have been in daily use for well over a hundred years; and museums in nearly all countries display old carpets, many of them dating back several hundred years, which have seen heavy wear over the centuries yet are still in excellent condition.

Kilims on Knotted Rugs

A carpetmaker will sometimes weave a plain kilim border at the top and bottom of a carpet. This may be made either of the wool of which the main background of the carpet is composed, or of cotton of the same material as the warps and wefts. An exceptionally long example is illustrated in Plate 44.

A large kilim on a carpet is mainly found in nomadic production and as the weaver is usually making the piece for himself or his family he does this extra work in order to strengthen the piece, though its absence does not necessarily denote an inferior quality.

Sometimes the man making the carpet will weave a small pattern in the kilim, either of diamonds or more generally of plain lines of wool in alternate colours. A good weaver, and one who is particularly keen on his work and on the standard of his craftsmanship, will frequently weave most attractive and large kilims. (The best such woven work is to be found in Beloudj.) This is, therefore, frequently the mark of a good carpet, because it is not normal practice for a weaver to be paid for this part of his work, any more than the ultimate buyer will be charged for it when purchasing a carpet from a shop. The kilim is surprisingly hard-wearing and will generally last nearly as long as the carpet although it is little thicker than a flannel shirt.

Irregularities

In making the knots the weaver on a vertical loom will pull them downwards to make them as tight as possible. On a horizontal loom the nomad will pull the knots towards himself. The result of this will be seen when the piece is finished in that the pile does not stand up vertically but lies a little towards the end where the work started.

By rubbing a flat hand over the pile it is always possible to see at which end the work was started, the end known as the front of the piece. The back is the end where the work finished.

A piece examined from the front always seems darker than from the back because of the minute shadows cast by the end of every single fibre; from the back these tiny shadows are largely hidden by the fibres themselves.

Some of the rug production in Persia is made with two pieces touching side by side on wide looms. When the two rugs are finished they are taken off the loom and then cut separate with a razor blade. The effect of this is that the weft is not continuous on one side and it has no loops to which the corded selvedge can be attached. The side cord is therefore merely sewn on as best as can be, and after a few years' use may pull off which is a source of weakness and irritation.

Babies and Mats and some of the Dozars from Karaja are made end to end, in other words one after the other, by setting a loom up with two, three or four lengths of warp. A space, sometimes very small, is left between the pieces, and when the work has been finished the unwoven part of the warps between the pieces is cut with a pair of scissors, leaving two normal fringed rugs quite as strong as if they had been separately made – stronger, in fact, than in side-by-side production.

As the work proceeds there is a great tendency for the weaver to pull the wefts tighter and tighter with the result that a small piece like a rug will often be found to have a waist. The two cross pieces at each end of the loom will hold the warps apart and thus ensure that they are not pulled together too much, but towards the middle, if the warps are a little too loose, they can close up noticeably. Sometimes to get round this difficulty the weaver will nail the warps as the work proceeds, but usually only at one side, with the result that one side will be straight whilst the other will curve inwards even more.

Larger pieces are usually wound on to the starting cross piece so as to keep the work at the same level as the worker, who usually sits on a plank some two or three feet off the ground. In this case the work gradually gets tighter and tighter towards the far end of the piece, and when a 10ft piece is taken off the loom its width may be as much as 2 or 3 inches more at the front, where the work started, than at the back.

Sometimes a piece has a bump down one side; sometimes it has quite a noticeable bump at the same place on both sides and is known as a bottle-shaped rug. This generally indicates that the work was stopped for a little while, perhaps for some religious festival or a marriage or birth or funeral in the family, and when resumed the worker had new enthusiasm; perhaps a different worker took it on, and his tension was completely different.

Another irregularity is for the colour of a carpet to change slightly, usually in a band running across the width. This effect, known as abradj, is of course the result of using a new batch of freshly dyed wool. The wool may have matched the previous batch perfectly when first used, but as both dye and wool were different it may fade or tone at a different rate from the original and abradjs will slowly appear. This is not regarded as a fault, but rather as a sign that the piece is genuinely handmade in the home or in a small-scale workshop; indeed, some machine-made carpets even introduce this effect intentionally in their oriental designs to try to give them a genuine appearance. If not too pronounced an abradj enhances the appearance of a real rug.

The Backs of Carpets

It is very interesting to turn a piece over and examine the workmanship from the back. It will be quite easily seen how many people have worked on each piece from the different patterns the knots make.

Making a carpet is very much like knitting. Two women can knit exactly the same pattern with the same wool and needles, but if they exchange their work in the middle it will be found that the tension is quite different. The same is true of carpets and is one of the hallmarks of a handmade piece.

Some people ask about the number of knots per square inch or per square cm. It is impossible to answer, as the number will vary widely both from side to side and from end to end of each piece. The only exceptions to this are some of the current workshop goods from Persia, Russia and China, but even they will be nowhere near as even as a machine-made carpet.

Sometimes from the back the pattern of knots appears to take the shape of a 'V' on its side, the narrow end pointing towards the centre of the carpet and opening out to the edge. This happens when a weaver has found that he has been making bigger knots one side of the carpet than the other – usually due to the fact that two skeins of wool are being used and as the wool is handspun one skein contains thicker wool than the other. The weaver can see this quite easily for himself as the design appears to start going round the corner and the only way he can correct it (if he is interested) is to insert a few lines of additional wefts across the carpet in order to fill up the space and thus get the pattern straight again. The 'V' comes as more additional wefts have to be added at the side of the piece than in the middle.

None of these peculiarities are defects, nor do they affect the strength, wearing quality or value of a piece in any way. A slight irregularity is the sign of a handmade carpet. A buyer of an oriental carpet who wishes to have a piece which is absolutely perfect in every respect, from the evenness of the stitch on the back to its shape, would be far better advised to purchase something which has been made by machine.

Much of the attraction of an oriental carpet comes from its very irregularity. It is fascinating when each piece is examined individually to see how the design varies across the carpet and from end to end. There are subtle changes in design, colour and shade and it is sometimes not until a piece has been at home for years that you even notice that the weaver went wrong in one place and made the design the wrong way round or upside down.

Warps and Wefts

From the back it is also possible to study the material of the warp and weft. As we have seen, this used to be of wool, but is now usually of cotton. The purist, when he has the option, tends to choose a piece knotted on a woollen warp and weft rather than on cotton. This is partly because the all-woollen piece is probably older, but also because the woollen warp and weft is softer, acting as a kind of underfelt prolonging the life of the carpet, while the cotton foundation is harder and less springy. Not many pieces are now made with woollen warp and weft, though these are still used in nearly all those from Afghanistan, both Afghans and Beloudj, most from Shiraz (other than some Luristans), most Turkomen pieces and some Meshed Beloudj.

The ends of the warp constitute the fringe. Unfortunately when most carpets are finished the fringes are not knotted; so the fringes should be oversewn before being put into use. Also, some carpets and rugs, particularly from the Hamadan region, have what is called a 'closed fringe' at the front, which means that the carpet was started with an inch or so of kilim on the bottom roller of the loom; in this case there will be no fringe at one end of the carpet.

On some pieces, again from the Hamadan region, diagonal lines 2 to 12in (5 to 30cm) long can be seen on the back. This is produced when two weavers work on one carpet and one of them works faster than the other. Instead of waiting to take his weft to the other side of the carpet, the faster weaver returns to his selvedge and starts another row. To prevent a vertical slit appearing in the middle of the carpet, as he finishes this new row his point of return must be two warps sooner. Equally, when his partner works this row he must continue two warps further to meet the finished part of the row. As this continues up the piece it creates the diagonal line, which particularly on old pieces, can become a source of weakness.

Silk Carpets

Silk has sometimes been used for carpets; the effect is often very fine and such pieces fetch high prices, but care must be taken in choosing a silk rug. Sometimes the warp and weft are silk; this gives a strong and very thin yarn, as fewer strands are required for the same length as silk fibres are longer than those of cotton. Sometimes silk is used in the knots to highlight some special effect, as for instance the petals of a flower, but as silk does not wear as well as wool the silk knots will tend to wear down with the years, giving an embossed effect which can be quite pleasing. Some rugs, again, are knotted entirely in silk. It must always be remembered that silk not only wears more quickly than wool but that it rots more quickly also; many people have the experience of discovering that a lovely silk dress or veil of their grandmother's crumbles away when touched today. In recent years artificial silk, which is mercerised cotton, has been used for some rugs, especially in Turkey.

As well as silk, gold and silver thread has sometimes been used in conjunction with an embossed wool pile in some luxury carpets. In the other direction, cotton has occasionally been used for the pile. This is normally regarded as a fault, because it looks too white and hard, quite lacking the soft feel and patina of white wool, but in some carpets where a very white effect is desired cotton has been used legitimately and effectively in the knotting. This would be particularly appropriate in pieces of sombre hues, where 'white' wool would become grey too soon, notably in old Turkomen goods such as the Russian Hatchli illustrated in Plate 44.

Washing Carpets

We have already mentioned that carpets are normally washed before being put on sale. This tends to improve the feel and soften the colours of a newly woven carpet and has no harmful effects, but there are two special kinds of washing of which carpet buyers should be aware.

Gold washing is a method of bleaching the red out of carpets and turning it into a silver, or more usually a gold, colour. The method was discovered at about the time of World War I; it was originally used only on Afghans, but in recent years it has been very extensively applied to carpets of all qualities. The effect is certainly pleasing and is sometimes fashionable, but purchasers of gold-washed carpets should realise that the process must take a lot out of the carpet and that its life is being shortened. Provided the buyer understands this, there need be no objection to it. It must, however, also be said that many gold-washed pieces have a tendency to lose, after a very few years' wear, what sheen they originally had, and will often look quite dead. A gold-washed carpet cannot be resold for as much money as it would have fetched if untreated.

The other kind of special washing is old or antique washing. This has the effect of artificially ageing a piece, and giving it the soft tones that normally come after many years of wear. There is a great demand for old and antique carpets, the supply is limited and getting less every month, so this method of washing obviously has its attractions. When well done, the effect is very pleasing and after a few years it will need a real expert to tell an old-washed carpet from a genuine old piece. The resale value is not affected in the same way as with gold washing, but it must be realised that the process does take some of the body out of the wool and shorten the life of the carpet.

An honest and reputable dealer will always tell you if a carpet has been treated with any of these artificial washes, but unfortunately a regular industry in fabricating antique carpets is now developing. These imitations are being manufactured in eastern Europe and then put on sale through various channels in western Europe and America. Not only are modern carpets being old-washed, but they are then being worn down by machines and stained by wild dogs, then repaired badly; and this being done so effectively that from five or ten yards even an expert cannot recognise them as brand-new.

The designs treated in this way are usually Caucasian, and would be very expensive indeed if they were genuine. These imitations are sold at dramatically cheaper prices, and there would, of course, be no objection at all to such goings-on if the carpets were sold as reproduction pieces. It is because many are passed off as genuine antiques that buyers must be on their guard.

7 Buying a Carpet

Buying a carpet is like buying any other article. You will only get what you pay for. As with many other kinds of goods, there is very little difference in appearance between the cheap and the expensive article when new; a cheap new suit can hang as well as one from Savile Row, but after even one or two years there will be all the difference in the world. In the same way, it is only when a carpet has been in use for a few months, or even a few years, that the difference between the good quality and the poor quality will become apparent.

Because of the increased demand for oriental carpets some firms have been advertising them at cut prices as though they were export-reject grade. As one of the main reasons for buying an oriental carpet is that it holds its value, it is most surprising these days that there are still people to be found who can be caught by clever newspaper advertisements offering carpets at reduced prices. No one should think that a carpet bought for 'half price' in a cut-price offer will be of the same quality and give the same wear as one bought for the full price from a reputable establishment.

Unless there is something inherently wrong with a carpet or rug there is no need for a shop to make more than modest reductions even during Sale times and then only because the Oriental Carpet Department has to follow the pattern set by all the other departments in the shop.

The fact that a shop may have had a piece in stock for one or two years does not reduce its worth, in fact it has probably increased in value. It merely means that that particular piece has not yet found the right home because its colour or its design or perhaps its size have not suited the customers who have seen it, but there is no piece yet made which has not got the right room waiting for it, one it will suit to perfection.

It is, of course, possible to purchase both oriental and machine-made carpets at public auctions. These are, basically, of three kinds.

First there are the regular auctions of carpets held by the leading auctioneers for art and antiques; Christie's and Sotheby Parke Bernet, for example, usually include carpets in a sale one day every week. These sales are attended mainly by trade buyers, and though there is nothing to prevent a private individual from bidding it is really not wise for him to do so unless he has a fairly expert knowledge of carpets and their current values. The entries in the auctioneer's catalogues are often very detailed, even if not all experts would always agree with their ascriptions, but they are written in technical terms that may mean little to a layman; moreover, the conditions on viewing days are such that it is often very difficult to examine a carpet properly. The actual procedure of bidding at a trade auction is very quick and can be confusing to any one unaccustomed to it; and even at a trade auction it cannot be assumed that prices will be lower than those being asked in retail shops at the same time.

Secondly, there are auctions held, usually in the country, at houses where all the contents are being sold. Such rare opportunities lure in every one in the district: certainly, bargains can sometimes be picked up, but equally certainly the dealers of the district will turn up too, and even though 'rings' are illegal they obviously will not allow a private buyer to walk away with a fine carpet for a song. Indeed, private buyers in the excitement of the auction not infrequently bid much more than they ever intended to, much more than similar objects can be bought for in shops.

Thirdly, there are the special exhibitions and auctions of carpets, sometimes advertised in glowing terms and often held in hotels. These are not intended for trade buyers, who don't go near them, but for the public, and – it must be said – for a public that is not necessarily well informed regarding carpet qualities and carpet values. It may, of course, be possible to buy a good quality carpet for a reasonable sum at such auctions; but the bulk of the pieces offered are, in fact, often of Pakistani, Romanian or Bulgarian origin, though the stress in the advertising will be upon the collector's pieces from Persia and the Caucasus; such fine Persians or old Caucasians as are offered will often be at higher prices than obtain for comparable pieces in ordinary shops. A carpet is an investment that will outlast your lifetime, and it is too important and too expensive a purchase for it to be made in the excitement of the moment or without careful thought and comparison of values.

A final story to illustrate how everything bought at auction is not necessarily a bargain. Not long ago a carpet sold by a leading department store began to show excessive wear after a very short time. The piece was returned, and a full refund was given without question. What was the shop to do with this piece? It put it into an auction, where it was bought by a private buyer at a price higher than the original retail price!

The best advice for any one thinking of buying a carpet is only to go to reputable shops which will give at least a moral guarantee that the piece is sound and good value for money. Most of the specialist carpet shops and leading department stores will give this. The buyer, too, should see for himself whether the salesman speaks with knowledge and whether he has confidence (but not over-confidence) in what he is selling. Does the salesman know one quality from another? Or does he have each time to refer to the price tag to find the name of the carpet or rug? (He must be expected, however, to look at the tag for the price, as every piece will be different.)

The price asked will depend, to some extent, upon the district from which the piece comes. Carpets and rugs from some areas have a high reputation, and this will be reflected in the price. But the wise buyer will look not just for a name but for quality and value for money. The best buy is often an outstanding example from a normally cheap range, rather than a run-of-the-mill example from a well-known area. In a way, carpets could be compared to various dishes of beef on the menu of a restaurant: steak is normally regarded as the best form of beef and is certainly the most expensive; a hamburger is regarded as quite inferior and is certainly cheaper; a connoisseur of good food would be expected to prefer the steak, if he could afford it, but any connoisseur would far rather have an excellent, well-cooked hamburger than a tough, leathery bit of steak. In the same way, a discerning buyer will look for a good piece from a cheap quality, or district, rather than a middle-grade piece from a more expensive quality.

Comparing one quality of carpet with another is a difficult matter at any time. Is a good Keshan better than a good Kirman? One might as well ask if chocolate is better than toffee. It is largely a matter of taste; what is certain is that good toffee is better than bad chocolate. So the buyer should not be hypnotised by names.

The price of a carpet will depend upon a combination of factors, as well as the district: Size; quality of the wool; workmanship; quality of the warp and weft; fineness of the stitch; design; colour; general aspect; and defects.

In general, large carpets work out cheaper per square foot or square metre than smaller sizes. Some special sizes cost more relatively, and small rugs and mats from some districts which are particularly sought after can be far more expensive pro rata than a carpet or Dozar of the same quality and stitch.

The wool, which is not graded as it is at the large wool auctions in Australia or at the Wool Exchange in London, does vary and a difference in its quality or the length of the staple, will affect the life of a piece, and hence its price. The quality of the warp and weft can vary just as much as that of the wool, and this, too, can have a limited bearing on the price.

Workmanship does not much affect the price unless it is particularly bad, such as if the wool is badly sheared so that the face of the carpet is clearly seen to be uneven.

Persians particularly value pieces according to the fineness of the stitch, but a fine stitch combined with a poor design will have nowhere near the worth of a coarser piece with a really attractive design. The design, the colours used and the general aspect will together do more than any of the other items in establishing the price.

In considering the weight of a piece it must be examined to see whether this comes from the depth and thickness of the pile or from fillers. Weight alone is no guide to quality or price.

The design, colour and general aspect is a matter of personal taste, but as far as the other factors are concerned we return to the advice already given: place your trust in an established carpet shop or department store. It is in the seller's interest to look after that of the buyer, as the average buyer rarely furnishes a whole house at once and the carpet seller does rely very much on having really satisfied customers so that when they wish to buy another piece they will return to him.

An increasing number of newly established carpet shops offer a guarantee to repurchase a carpet at cost plus a given percentage (usually 10 per cent). Most well established firms would never make such an offer, as they cannot know what value a piece will have in one, two or ten years' time, nor could they guess its condition. Such an offer does not make sense from the shop's point of view as the original price would have included a share of the shop's overheads (particularly VAT which exceeds 20 per cent in some countries) and it would be re-buying at more than the gross price. It could be replaced from a wholesaler for much less. The shop is then faced with re-selling the piece without a profit, overpricing it to make a profit a second time, or, if prices have dropped, making a loss. Part exchange is quite different as little or no money changes hands.

As a further guide to choosing a carpet seller, look to see whether the shop has sufficient confidence in the goods to have them on the floor, to be walked on day after day and yet still be for sale. Look to see if the fringes have been oversewn, and the sides sewn out so that they lie quite flat. They will not flatten in use whatever a salesman may say. Check that none of the goods have tickets or labels attached with ordinary wire staples which may scratch, and which will certainly go rusty and so damage the carpet. Are the bulk of the carpets rolled up, or are the majority of pieces flat as they ought to be? Are all the pieces presented the same way round, so that the pile is the same way and the colours can be compared? Are they shown on a reasonably large, flat area, or presented in such a way that it is impossible to see whether the pieces are straight or flat, or have other faults? Are all the tickets with the details of size and price properly attached, in the same corner, or have they been attached haphazardly? Does the salesman handle the pieces as though they have value, or are they just thrown around and pulled aside as if they have none? Beware also of sellers who tell you that they will attend to a little hole after *you* have found it. There may be others which the vendor should first have found, and he should not wait for you to find a defect before mentioning it.

So, again, always buy from an established dealer and avoid those with continuous, or near continuous, sales or those offering large discounts or gimmicks.

8 Care and Repair

Up to a certain point the appearance of an oriental carpet improves with age and some people prefer to buy a carpet secondhand rather than new. If it has been well cared for in an American or European home its condition will still be excellent, though even here accidents can happen. If the carpet is bought secondhand in a Middle East country its condition may be rather poor. Many dealers in the East age their carpets artificially by leaving them out in the sun, putting them on the pavement for all the passers-by to walk over, or washing them in a solution of wood ash. Treatment like this may reduce the harshness of poor-quality aniline dyes but it is no way to bring up the beautiful patina of age. Even if nothing like this has been done, a used carpet from the Middle East is almost always stained and dirty.

Chairs have not yet come into use in the main carpet-producing regions and it is still normal practice to sit cross-legged on the floor of the tent, either on a half-filled saddle bag or actually on the carpet or rug. If a family lives in a tent the carpets and rugs will be placed on the ground; in many towns, the streets – even when they can aspire to such a high-sounding name – are little better than farm tracks, dusty in summer and wet and muddy in winter, so that most pieces get quickly dirty and stained as people walk in and out. Meals are taken and letter-writing is done on the carpet and we suspect that sometimes even internal-combustion engines are dismantled on good carpets and rugs. Greasy food will be spilt, and as letters are written with an ordinary dip pen from an open bottle of ink, the ink bottle will sometimes get spilt too. Some pieces will be found with a burn or the wool a little singed, as charcoal braziers are often used for cooking and a piece of burning charcoal is used to light the invariably dampened tobacco of a hookah (the rose-water pipe used all over the Middle East) and occasionally red-hot ashes and embers fall out on to the carpet. This cannot upset the owners, as no real effort seems ever to be made to prevent such accidents or to remove stains when they do occur.

Dirt, Stains and Burns

Regular vacuum cleaning is the best treatment for dirt in a carpet. If a brush is used, the direction of strokes should be with the lie of the pile, not against it. Beating should not be resorted to except in extreme cases, and then from the back, not on the front, and with a carpet beater, never a stick. Ingrained dirt may be removed with a carpet shampoo, but be very careful not to over-wet a piece and make sure it is thoroughly dried. This is particularly important with pieces woven with woollen warps and wefts, because if they get wet the piece may dry all crinkly.

Some stains can be removed by immediate treatment with a chemical cleaner, though this is liable to weaken the fibres. If necessary, a carpet can be washed but this is a skilled operation and should never be attempted at home; it should be entrusted to a firm specialising in this treatment, and not to the local dry-cleaner, who may inadvertently ruin it in his back yard. Old or valuable pieces really should be given to specialist dealers for hand cleaning, which while more expensive than machine cleaning is very strongly recommended. In general, small stains which are not very noticeable on an intricate design do not reduce the value of a carpet, but obviously a large ink stain on a plain, open ground will do so.

Burns can be quite invisibly repaired and a skilful repair will not affect the value of the carpet. Unfortunately good carpet repairers are hard to find; the best are Armenian or Jewish, and these days a few Pakistanis are really prepared to take the trouble to do a good job. Repairs in the country of origin are often badly executed; the Muslim belief that only Allah made anything that was perfect is a sad disincentive to good workmanship!

Tears

Carpets may get damaged or torn in use, or in transit which can be more serious, depending upon the extent of the damage.

They are sent from their countries of origin packed in fairly large bales weighing up to 4 or 5cwt, so dockers have to use 'hooks' to lift and move them. If a bale is particularly heavy or if it is awkwardly wedged at the bottom of the hold the hooks occasionally make a small tear. A hook hole or a small tear – unless it is in a plain open ground – can be so expertly repaired that it will be almost invisible and it will then not affect the worth, strength or wearing qualities of the carpet.

Rot

It was said in an earlier chapter that no carpets or rugs are sold well below their market value unless they have some inherent fault, and there is no doubt that many pieces offered at half-price and under cost are *chourouk*, which is a most serious defect. The word is Turkish and means that a piece is rotten or perished due to having got wet and not being dried out properly.

Very occasionally whole bales get wetted by seawater while in transit and the salts and acids in the water work on the warps and wefts until they rot. If the damage occurs at the end of a voyage, which is rare, and if the pieces are quickly and thoroughly washed and dried, no damage will have been done. Unfortunately when pieces get wet this usually occurs when they are embarked, as they are frequently loaded at sea from barges, and during the whole voyage the piece 'cooks' until on arrival it is quite *chourouk*.

When the cotton warps and wefts rot, they leave little visible sign. The carpet or rug may be a little stiffer there than elsewhere, but unless the buyer is prepared to bend a piece backwards and forwards all over to check this he will not know until the piece has been in use a few years. It will then begin to disintegrate at all the points where the piece is *chourouk*, just like any machine-made carpet which has been overwetted and dried too slowly. Because of the way carpets are folded when put into a bale for shipment no piece is normally *chourouk* all over. There may be six or eight damaged places, but only at the folds, so they tend to appear in two straight lines a third of the way in from each border of a carpet or along the centre fold of a rug.

When pieces are damaged in transit the owners, of course, receive compensation from their underwriters and the shop can then advertise the goods in question as 'half-price, slightly sub-standard' or with some other nebulous description that can hide a multitude of sins. It therefore pays to shun all 'half-price' advertisements unless covered by a written guarantee from a reputable dealer or store that the goods are perfect and that the piece is of identical quality and colour to pieces that can be bought currently elsewhere at double the price. The fact that it may have the same name proves nothing, as the cheapest quality may be worth only one-tenth of the price of the finest pieces produced in the same district. Some cheap offers are, of course, quite genuine. Recently there was a shipment of rugs that was so badly damaged by sea water that it sold for a song. The buyer cut out the rotten parts and joined the sound pieces together with canvas tape on the back and then sold the rugs for about one-tenth of their normal price. The buyers of these particular goods could see exactly what they were getting, which was quite fair; if only the sound parts of the rugs were used to make up these fragments, as they are called, they would last just as long as an undamaged piece.

Moth

Carpets and rugs are neither made of mothproofed wool nor treated to make them mothproof before sale. If kept clean, a piece should never become mothy, but in the Middle East where carpets are sometimes laid one on top of the other, the bottom one, which is being used more or less as a rather expensive underfelt, can get motheaten. In Europe and America heavy furniture like a bookcase or sideboard sometimes prevents a carpet from being properly cleaned and it may then get mothy.

Only the wool is attacked; the cotton warps and wefts are left untouched and they keep the piece together, so until it is moved or cleaned nothing will show. The damage is usually found on the back, where the female moth can lay her eggs in peace and the larvæ hatch. The dishonest cure for this is to paint the back where the wool has been eaten, and nothing will then show until a piece has been beaten and swept with a carpet sweeper for several months, when the wool will start falling out of the face of the carpet. If only the design is affected it does not matter too much; the piece can be baked to kill any moth eggs remaining and the design invisibly replaced. But if the damage is in a plain ground, the repair cannot be hidden as it is impossible to match the colour of the new wool to that of the undamaged part and even if it does not show from one end, it nearly always does from the other.

Bumps and Wrinkles

As the looms on which nomad and cottage carpets are made are not exactly rectangular, it is not surprising that the finished product is not rectangular either, and – unless it is very extreme – this does not affect its price in the least; but some pieces do not lie quite flat and they should be stretched, as otherwise the wool will wear at the bumps far faster than elsewhere, just as any carpet will if laid on a very uneven floor or as a stair carpet wears at the edge of each tread.

If, however, a piece does not lie flat because it has been creased in a bale, like a suit in a tightly packed trunk, the creases will frequently drop out. If they do not go within a year or so it also should be stretched to flatten it, as this will undoubtedly greatly prolong its life.

Curling Edges

Finely knotted pieces and those with a tight but long pile have a tendency to curl over at the edges because the individual wool staples are kept tightly together by the knot at the warps and wefts, but they open out near the surface causing the top to roll over the edge. If this happens, or if the carpet gets turned under in use, the side must be sewn down by a carpet repairer, which will ensure that it will lie flat for the rest of its life. Sticky tape is not recommended as this may reduce the value of a piece. Merely to iron a carpet or to sew cardboard on the back will not cure this or only do so temporarily. Always insist that any curling edges are sewn out before delivery from the shop, although it is normal practice for reputable dealers to see to this without being asked.

Cracked Pieces

Some pieces have had the wefts beaten down so hard that the carpet when finished is as stiff as a board. This has advantages, in as much as it lies nice and flat, but its greatest disadvantage comes when it is folded.

It is normal to fold a carpet inwards to keep the pile or face clean, but if this is done with a heavy or stiff carpet the warp and weft may crack, particularly on folding with four equal quarters or 'cross' folds. The correct way to fold any stiff carpet is to ensure that *all* folds are parallel, and if this is not possible the piece must be folded inside out, that is with the pile on the outside, care being taken to keep it clean; it can then be folded just like any other carpet.

These remarks apply to nearly all Bidjars, Sarouks and Afghans, many Baktyars, Keshans and Russians, and to some Kirmans and Sharibaffs as well as extra fine pieces like Nayin and Ispahan, and any other pieces that are hard and rigid.

If a warp or weft does get cracked, this can be repaired quite easily by sewing the threads together again: the rug may be no worse for its experience. Care must, however, be taken to see that this repair is carried out quickly, otherwise the crack may eventually develop into a hole which will be much more costly to repair.

General Care

It is always desirable to place an underlay under a carpet except those with a very thick pile. If heavy furniture is placed on the carpet the weight of the legs should be taken by additional supports; the position of the carpet, or of the furniture, should be changed from time to time to avoid crushing the pile. One reason why oriental carpets last so long is that they 'walk', that is shift slightly with use, so that they are not continually trodden on in exactly the same place; all the same, they should be turned at yearly intervals so as to spread the wear evenly from one end or side to the other. The most intense wear will come in a doorway, but by turning the carpet the wear is effectively halved as compared with that of a fitted carpet. Never nail a carpet to the floor, though of course if used on a staircase it must be fastened in this way; in this case, however, the carpet *must* be moved a little *every* year. A runner with bald stripes every 18in is almost valueless.

If the floor is damp it is essential to take the carpet up and leave it to dry with the underside up; water itself can do no harm to a carpet if it is quickly dried, but if mould is allowed to form the results can be serious. Carpets are meant to be walked on, and a normal amount of walking will do no harm at all but rubber soles can injure the fibres in the course of time. The fringe of a carpet is often the first place where wear and tear will show, but it is perfectly simple to have this attended to. If you have bought your carpet from a specialist dealer he will be glad to advise you about any repairs or treatment that may become necessary.

9 Carpets in the Home

Can an oriental carpet fit into the design of the modern home? Yes, of course, particularly as it is always the carpet that makes any room. However primitive the design of an oriental carpet may be, it suits the most modern of modern furniture as well as it does period furniture.

Modern furniture is attractive because of its clean and often straight lines; modern curtains and hangings and modern wallpapers are also attractive because of their uncluttered designs. But if all this is centred around a carpet with little or no pattern or colour the whole room looks far too cold and clinical. In such surroundings an oriental carpet brings life and warmth, to give at least the impression that a room is lived in and not just a show-place.

Just as a painting of a vase of flowers will hardly be seen to advantage against a flowered, patterned wallpaper, so one must not kill either a carpet or curtains by trying to reproduce the same design in both.

Colours

The oriental carpet shows to all with eyes to see how to play with colour in the furnishing of a room. There is no difficulty in choosing an oriental carpet to match any colour scheme, as the colours of the existing wallpaper and furnishings can be found and picked out in such a variety of designs; it will even be seen that colours at first thought to clash can lie side by side in harmony. Although the people who make these carpets are extraordinarily primitive they have a feeling for colour which goes back centuries, and they have even learnt instinctively how to blend blues with greens and the most beautiful reds with pinks.

As most oriental carpets have such a rich profusion of varied colours, they provide immediate suggestions on what new colour scheme to adopt when the time comes to change the wallpaper and repaint a room. In fact, they offer an almost unlimited variety of colours and shades so that a room can be easily changed every few years without once repeating the same theme.

Though the majority of Afghans have but two colours – various shades of red and very dark blue bordering almost on black – the choice they allow when it comes to redecoration is again almost unrestricted. It is hard to envisage any scheme of interior decoration which an Afghan carpet, with its simple design, cannot complement or improve. Similarly, most Chinese, apart from the very expensive types with French or Aubusson designs, also use few

41

colours, though with these, as with Kirmans, their main colour tends to dominate a room.

Placing

As neither the sides nor the ends of a handmade carpet are ever quite straight it is not desirable to have them too near a wall, as this will accentuate the little bump here and the little dent there. So when measuring a room for a carpet allow a margin all round of about 20 to 30 per cent of floor space which will help to frame the carpet and make it even more attractive. For example a room 16ft long and 12ft wide (5·00 × 3·60m) needs a carpet measuring about 12ft × 9ft (3·60 × 2·70m) and if there is a projecting hearth the carpet will fit fairly flush up to it. If it is desired to leave a space between the carpet and the hearth the right size would then be about 12ft × 8ft 6in (3·60 × 2·60m).

Acquiring

If one is restricted by price it is better not to try to stretch a given sum of money over the largest area but to purchase the smallest piece that will suit the room for the amount one can afford. A smaller piece will give a ruggish and frequently more striking effect; it will undoubtedly be of better quality than a larger piece at the same price and will, therefore, be a more interesting and a more valuable acquisition for the home.

If one becomes very attached to one of these fine small pieces and yet in years to come is wishing to cover more of the floor, it will not be difficult to purchase one or two small pieces to scatter round the room as, for example, do many Scandinavians.

Your first oriental carpet may only be a fairly inexpensive rug to go in front of the fire or in the hall, but after a while there will be a feeling of dissatisfaction with the other carpets in your house; you will wish to acquire a second and then a third and then a fourth piece, until every room in the house will be furnished with oriental carpets. Almost without knowing it, you will have become a collector of oriental carpets, and like any collector you will be able to develop your collection in many different ways. You may choose to acquire carpets from as many different districts as possible, so as to demonstrate the range and variety. Or you may prefer to limit your collection to carpets that all come from one district, but which illustrate the variations of design that can be found within it. Or you may merely choose carpets for the personal appeal that their design makes to you, without bothering where they come from. You will almost certainly change your rugs and carpets from room to room from time to time; even turning a carpet round, so that the lie of the pile is at a different angle to the direction of light from the window, can make a surprising difference to its appearance; putting it in a different room can transform the appearance of the room – or of the carpet.

If your finances improve and you find that you are able to acquire better and better carpets, you may wish to replace the one in your lounge, for instance. Ideally you might now move the old carpet from the lounge to another room, but even if it will not fit elsewhere the problem is not difficult.

If it is a real oriental carpet, you can take it back to the shop from which it was originally bought, where you will receive a very high part-exchange allowance, however long the piece has been in use.

Over the course of time you will have acquired a really pleasing collection of beautiful handmade carpets which can be handed on from generation to generation.

Starting with kilims

Good carpets are, naturally, expensive, but there is no need to imagine that collecting them is only for millionaires. One type of carpet that can be bought relatively inexpensively, and is very popular today, is the kilim.

These smooth rugs are very versatile. Their colours and design suit modern furnishings, and they can be used not only on the floor but as bedspreads, on tables, armchairs and settees, and hanging on the wall. A kilim has even been found useful to cover up an incurable damp patch on a wall! They are hard wearing, and as their appearance is exactly the same on both sides, they can be turned over if the colours on one side have faded, to give wear on both sides. Because they are not as bulky as carpets with a pile, they can be stored, flat or rolled up, in very little space. As this might be a good type of carpet to start off a collection, and as it fits so well into the modern home, it may be useful to give here a little additional information about kilims.

The main centres of production at the present time are in Turkey and Persia. The Turkish kilims come in two main sizes: 6ft × 4ft (1·80 × 1·20m), the majority of which are prayer designs, and large ones measuring between 12ft and 16ft (3·00 and 5·00m) long by 6ft to 8ft (1·80 to 2·45m) wide. The colours of the large Turkish kilims tend to be better than those of the small ones, especially in old examples; this may be because the large carpets got more use, which up to a point improves the appearance of any good carpet, while the small ones used to be kept for dowries and remained rolled up until a marriage could be arranged. These large carpets are generally made in two pieces on two fairly narrow looms, and then sewn together down the middle. The design usually consists of a series of diamond-shaped medallions, and unfortunately the size of the diamonds, and even the length of carpet, in the two halves do not always match; often the differences are not too great and the result is acceptable, but sometimes the two halves are glaringly out of match. You would have to be a real enthusiast for collecting Turkish kilims to buy something that was apparently so badly out of shape!

Persian kilims come mainly from Shiraz, though today quite a number are coming from Veramin, and the finest still come, as they have always done, from Sine. The Shiraz and the Veramin tend to use simple, primitive geometric designs; the Veramin particularly look very Caucasian now, and many people take them for Kazaks. The Sines invariably have very fine designs, and for these beautiful rugs the rule that kilims are inexpensive can no longer apply; for the finest pieces the prices have increased enormously.

43

10 Carpets as an Investment

Faced with the problem of world inflation, many people are realising that the best investment they can make with any money they may have is to buy articles of use and beauty that are likely to maintain, or even increase, their value with the years. Such investments may pay no dividends in cash, but they give continuous pleasure while they are lived with and show no loss of real capital if they have to be sold. This principle, however, applies only to articles of good or first-class quality; if you are buying for investment the golden rule is to buy the very best that you can afford.

After a house to live in, furnishings for the house must come next in importance, and among such furnishings good carpets rank very high. A carpet that is bought with an eye to investment as well as for its immediate practical use should be long-wearing and have a design that will not seem out of date after a few years. Real oriental carpets meet these requirements. Their wonderful designs and glorious colours have delighted countless people over the centuries, perhaps because they were the products of such simple, primitive folk and the way in which they have been combined never ceases to amaze and mystify students of art. There is, however, a small but increasing production of oriental carpets with modern designs and colours, and of these an investor should beware, as they are not likely to be so sought after or so desirable when one comes to sell them many years later, when passing 'contemporary' tastes will have changed.

A real handmade oriental carpet is an altogether better investment than a machine-made carpet. It is far longer lasting; its life is five, ten or twenty times that of a machine-made carpet while its price is not all that high in comparison. Indeed it has been said with truth that a good modern oriental carpet will last as long as a good average modern house.

By giving a real carpet intensive use over the course of time, the wool will gradually get polished and the natural oils will come to the surface, giving it a most wondrous sheen. In fact, an old piece will, on examination, sometimes look as though it is made of pure silk although it contains only virgin wool.

When it is new its colours can be a little bright, even though vegetable dyes may have been used, but they soften over the years and the demand in Europe and America for pieces with the softer colourings found in old goods is almost insatiable. Because many people are unwilling to buy a carpet and use it themselves in order to bring out this wonderful lustre, old, used, secondhand pieces fetch high prices, often higher than when new. The only qualification is, of course, that the piece should be evenly worn all over. How much it is worn is not very important as long as the design still remains; even when the cotton warps and wefts can be seen all over, a piece will still look attractive and will not have lost all its value; it will have become very suitable for use with genuine antique furniture.

Pieces which have been unevenly worn, however, with a bald patch in one place, are of little value. They do not attract the buyers of either a new carpet or an old one, and however cheap are of no value as an investment. Similarly, it is not good policy to buy a damaged piece, even if it comes from a highly regarded district; any imperfection will always reduce the value of a piece, so a damaged carpet is always a bad investment. If goods of this kind are avoided, however, an oriental carpet can be purchased and used for ten, twenty or thirty years, and at the end of that time be worth at least as much and frequently more than the original cost price, even after allowing for monetary inflation.

One big qualification must be made, however. The carpets which will really keep their value are only the 'real oriental carpets', those that come from Persia, Afghanistan and Russia and perhaps from Turkey. Frankly, this principle does not normally apply to the products of other lands. It is interesting to note that in specialist carpet shops, department stores and even wholesale warehouses, the real carpets in use on the floor are for sale at full price, while if any of the other group are to be found they are only there for display as fixtures and fittings and not for sale. The suppliers of these goods confirm this difference by their own actions.

Nevertheless, not all 'real' carpets have investment value. For example, open ground, light and cream-coloured pieces, which come mainly from Kirman, Tabriz, Keshan and Koum, will soon become dirty and lose their appeal and value.

But these are not particularly expensive items; a far worse investment could be a fine Nayin or Hereke or silk Koum, among the finest, silkiest and costliest carpets and rugs manufactured today. These two qualities are particularly promoted by new carpet shops and stores, who often know little or nothing about oriental carpets, and are able to rely upon their silkiness or fineness to make a sale. Of course opinions differ as to their investment status, but neither at warehouse nor at retail level are these goods left on the floor to be walked on (any more than are new Chinese, Bulgarians, Pakistanis or Indo-Persians). The reason is that once 'shop-soiled' their value falls, and if their shop value falls with wear, what will happen when they are used in the home? By contrast other 'real' carpets are invariably displayed so that they can be walked on by all and sundry.

With the drop in the value of money the difference between the selling price today and the cost price of the same piece a few years ago is quite startling. Many carpet shops have, in fact, repurchased pieces which have been used for twenty and thirty years at five and ten times their original cost price. We would not, however, wish to mislead readers by suggesting that this is going to happen every twenty or thirty years (though soaring world inflation could make the increase even greater). No one should expect to make a quick profit from buying and selling carpets; a real carpet is essentially a medium-term investment.

It must also be remembered that the standard of living in Persia is steadily increasing, and the weavers there are improving their lot. And, almost more important, the children who used to make so many of Persia's finest pieces now go to school and are lost for several years to the labour market. For how long will they be content to go in for carpet weaving, after a more formal education? The result of all this is that the cost of production is rising rapidly and, like oil, carpets from Persia are going to cost much more than they used to.

Then, with the increase and the wider spread of wealth throughout the world, more people have the money available to buy carpets that are frequently almost works of art. This vastly increasing demand, coupled with only a limited increase in production, has also caused an increase in price.

A point worth bearing in mind is that no two nomadic or cottage carpets are quite identical. Should your carpet ever be stolen you would be able easily to identify it, even many years later, from among a pile of several hundred, if you have taken the precaution of having it photographed or, at least, recording a full description of it.

Finally some people may think that they will tire of the design of their carpet in a few years. Only rarely is this true; the design of a real oriental carpet seems to present new facets as the years go by, partly because of its very irregularity. In the last resort, however, as has been said, it is the easiest thing in the world to take one of these carpets back to the shop from which it came and part-exchange it for another piece.

The best way to find out more about oriental carpets is to look at and handle as many as possible. Following the illustrations there are lists of the best known museum collections and also some useful books. When looking at carpets in museums, make your own analysis of the design and estimate its type and age before looking at the label. Even if you are wrong, remember that the experts sometimes differ.

The best thing of all is to talk about carpets as often as possible. Carpet dealers are almost always ready to talk to a serious student, even if not an immediate purchaser, partly because an enthusiast may one day have the means to buy, but most of all because no one can sell, buy or live with oriental carpets without wanting to spread the knowledge and love of these beautiful objects.

Notes to Illustrations

1 Avshar Zaronim   4ft 11in × 3ft 6in (1·50 × 1·07m)
A fine contemporary piece which has yet not lost all its spontaneity. In fact it contains many quirks; for example in the space between the first and second medallions is a whole Serabend motif on the right, whereas on the left is only a half motif. Many similar quirks can be found upon close study. A typical Avshar border. (Collection Mrs G. Izmidlian)

2 Baktyar Dozar   6ft 11in × 4ft 8in (2·11 × 1·42m)
A typical contemporary piece of garden design showing the Maj-Nun (weeping willow) on cream ground and cypress trees on red ground, as well as other floral motifs. A piece of more than average character as it is not completely symmetrical. Typical Baktyar colour and design

3 Detail of Baktyar Dozar (Plate 2): the Maj-Nun and cyprus-tree motifs

4 Meshed Beloudj Rug   6ft 9in × 3ft 5in (2·06 × 1·04m)
A typical example of one of the most common of Beloudj designs, in this instance a sort of Feraghan motif. The central diamond can be readily seen, but the four palm leaves have become very large indeed and have joined together on each side to become huge horizontal Vs. Meshed Beloudj can generally be judged by the number of borders (the more borders the better; though of course fine pieces are also made with few borders, coarse pieces are never made with many) and this piece has eight at each end, but nine at each side. Note the fineness of the two 'S' borders and of the two borders with roses

5 Feraghan Dozar   7ft × 4ft 2in (2·13 × 1·27m)
A nice 60 to 70 year-old piece with a typical elaborate Feraghan design showing an adaptation of the Allah-Allah design. The borders are very typical of Feraghan. A piece worthy of closer study

6 Hamadan Dozar   7ft 6in × 4ft 7in (2·29 × 1·40m)
A typical modern Dozar in colour, size and design, but modern Hamadan Dozars tend to be 10–20 per cent larger than the pre-war production. This piece has a Begardeh type of design with stylized floral motifs

7 Heriz Dozar   6ft 6in × 4ft 11in (1·98 × 1·50m)
A typical modern Heriz with a good medallion and well-composed corners. Dozars made in Heriz are wider than average

8 Ispahan Baby   3ft 3in × 2ft 1in (0·99 × 0·64m)
A beautifully composed design, typical of the Safavid period. Similar scroll work can be found at the base of pillars in the Vakil mosque in Shiraz. A very fine piece woven on pure silk warp and weft, and yet even in such a fine piece a pronounced Abradj can be seen in the red of the border. Knotted fringe. (Collection Mrs G. Izmidlian)

9 Keshan Dozar   7ft 1in × 4ft 6in (2·16 × 1·37m)
A very interesting medallion as it is more round than the usually elongated shape found in Keshans, which is more pointed at each end and usually twice as long as it is wide. The main design is good, consisting not merely of numerous single large flowers, but of many

groups of small flowers growing from a single stem. The main border and guard stripes are typical Keshan and as the guard stripes are so often of identical design, they are a great help in comparing the quality of one piece with another

10 Detail of Keshan (Plate 9): showing the rather rounded medallion and the groups of small flowers, some white and some dark blue

11 Fine Figural Kirman Mat   2ft 9in × 1ft 11in (0·84 × 0·58m)
By far the finest piece illustrated in this book and typical of what many call Laver Kirman, where the finest work has often been lavished on very artistic figural rugs. An interesting feature of this piece is that on each person is an Arabic numeral which refers back to the cartouches in the border and gives their names. (Collection Mrs G. Izmidlian)

12 Kirman Dozar   7ft 1in × 4ft 7in (2·16 × 1·40m)
Typical of today's production. A good blaze medallion on open ground, the main feature being the small bunches of flowers which go out from the medallion and corners onto the red ground, very typical of better quality Kirmans

13 Part-Silk Koum Zaronim   5ft 4in × 3ft 7in (1·62 × 1·09m)
Typical modern production of a mixture of wool and silk, but with more silk than usual, particularly in the bodies of the animals. People and animals have been fairly faithfully portrayed, something to look for in similar pieces. Note the additional dog-tooth border up both sides adjacent to the ground which helps to give this piece a little more individuality

14 Detail of Koum: a good example of an elaborate Serabend or Mir-Boteh design

15 Old Mecca Shiraz Baby   3ft 11in × 2ft 7in (1·19 × 0·79m)
Unusual size for a Mecca Shiraz, the majority being either Dozars or saddle bags. A typical nomadic rug, which merits study as its very irregularity gives it charm and character. The design started at the bottom with some symmetry, but this was soon completely lost. In the central area, the typical Mecca Shiraz motif and the diamond beyond are surrounded by reasonably symmetrical motifs, but after that all semblance of balance is again lost. This was almost certainly made as a sampler. (Collection Mrs G. Izmidlian)

16 Mouchakar Dozar   7ft 11in × 4ft 9in (2·41 × 1·45m)
Today Mouchakar Dozars are very large, almost small 8 × 5s (2·50 × 1·50m), and this is a good example of contemporary production. In the cheaper qualities, however, the diagonal lines of motifs tend to run right through the medallion, giving the rug a machine-made effect, whereas in this instance the designs in the medallion have changed and do not fit into the ground motif where many of the designs have had to be cut into. The main border is very typical. The innermost and outermost guard stripes are the same as those to be found in many fine Keshans. A close study of this piece will reveal an interesting interpretation of the Maj-Nun (weeping willow) design

17 Fine Sarouk Dozar   6ft 5in × 4ft 2in (1·96 × 1·27m)
An unusually fine Sarouk with particularly attractive medallion and corners. Note the very long tendrils in the ground and the fine cartouches in the border, particularly the bunch of three roses in the corners of the main border. The inside and outside guard stripes are, however, typically Keshan. (Collection Mrs L. D. Futerman)

18 Detail of Sarouk Dozar (plate 17): clearly shows the fine design of this piece. Note the attractive cartouches and the way in which they have been worked in the corner of the main border

19 Semi-old Afghan Rug   7ft × 3ft 4in (2·13 × 1·02m)
A very nice specimen with stepped gul Pendik design and very clear borders. Note the small Serabend-like motifs in the two wider guard stripes, and the fact that the weaver began to run out of warp and was therefore only able to complete a quarter of a motif before starting the top border

1 Avshar Zaronim 4ft 11in x 3ft 6in (1.50 x 1.07m)

2 Baktyar Dozar 6ft 11in x 4ft 8in (2.11 x 1.42m)

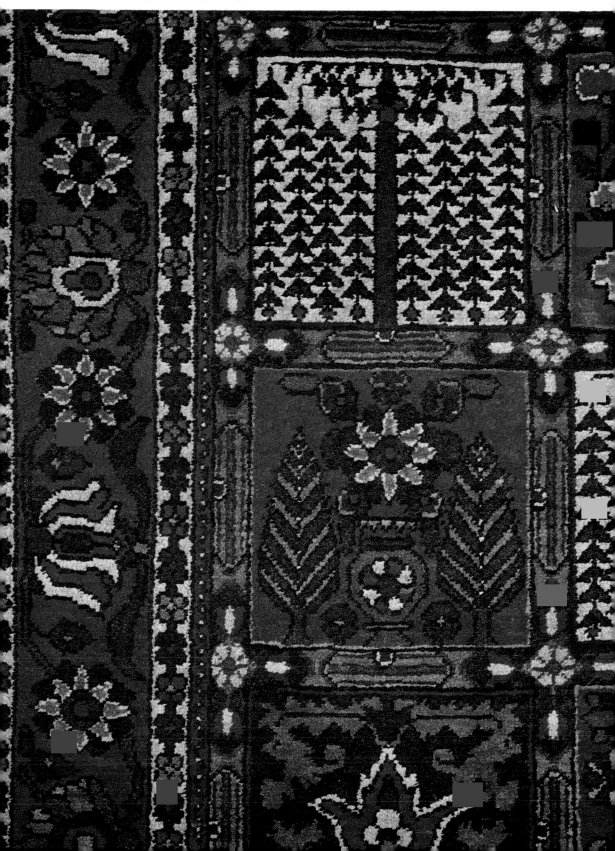

3 **Detail of Baktyar Dozar** (Plate 2)

4 Meshed Beloudj Rug 6ft 9in x 3ft 6in (2.06 x 1.04m)

5 **Feraghan Dozar** 7ft x 4ft 2in (2.13 x 1.27m)

6 **Hamadan Dozar** 7ft 6in x 4ft 7in (2.29 x 1.40m)

8 Ispahan Baby 3ft 3in x 2ft 1in (0.99 x 0.64m)

9 Keshan Dozar 7ft 1in x 4ft 6in (2.16 x 1.37m)

12 Kirman Dozar 7ft 1in x 4ft 7in (2.16 x 1.40m)

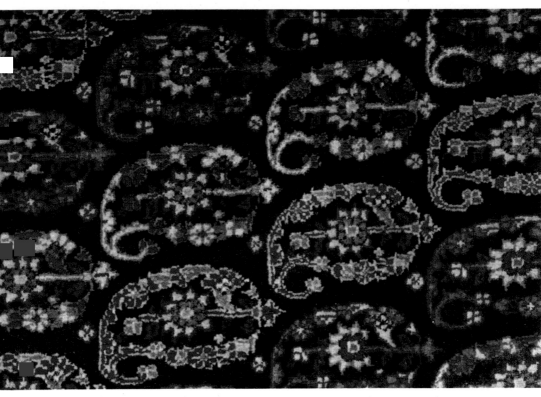

13 **Part-Silk Koum Zaronim** 5ft 4in x 3ft 7in (1.62 x 1.09m)

14 Close up of a Mir design

15 Old Mecca Shiraz Baby 3ft 11in x 2ft 7in (1.19 x 0.79m)

16 **Mouchakar Dozar** 7ft 11in x 4ft 9in (2.41 x 1.45m)

17 **Fine Sarouk Dozar** 6ft 5in x 4ft 2in (1.96 x 1.27m)

18 **Detail of Sarouk Dozar** (Plate 17)

19 Semi-old Afghan Rug 7ft × 3ft 4in (2.13 × 1.02m)

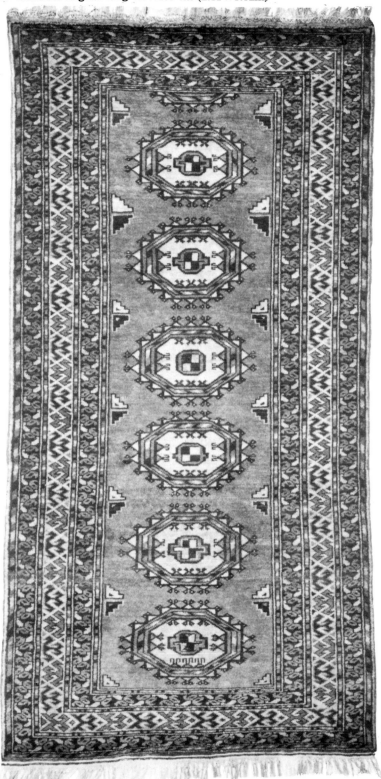

20 Antique Afghan Beshire 7ft 6in × 4ft 1in (2.30 × 1.25m)

22 Avshar Dozar 7ft 4in × 5ft 2in (2.23 × 1.57m)

23 Semi-old Baktyar Dozar 6ft 5in × 4ft 4in (1.96 × 1.32m)

24 Semi-old Russian Bokara Rug 5ft 6in × 3ft 10in (1.68 × 1.17m)

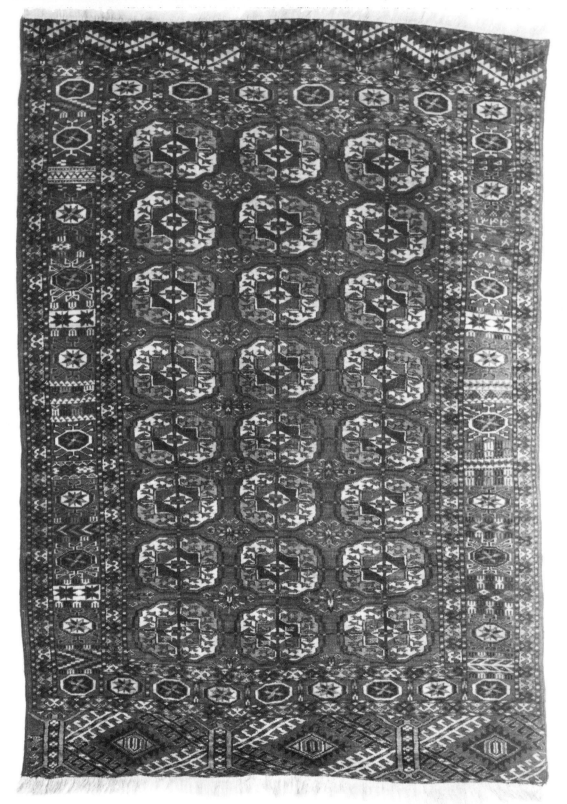

26 **Semi-old Ispahan Dozar** 6ft 10in × 4ft 11in (2.08 × 1.50m)

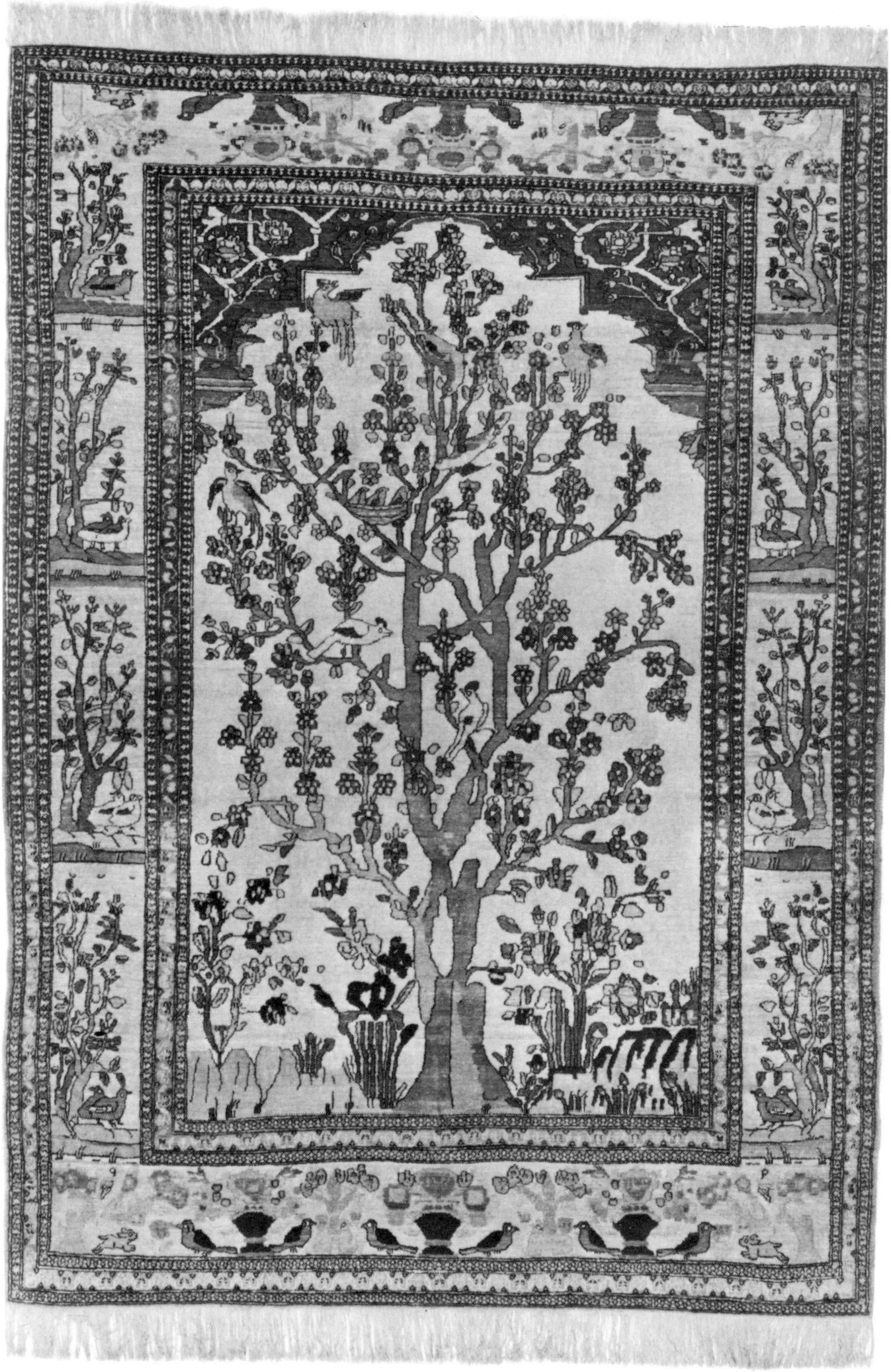

27 Semi-old Keshan Dozar 6ft 5in × 3ft 6in (1·96 × 1·07m)

28 **Kirman Dozar** 7ft 9in × 4ft 6in (2.36 × 1.37m)

30 Moud Dozar 6ft 6in × 4ft 5in (1.98 × 1.35m)

31 Sarap Mossul 6ft 6in × 3ft 3in (2.00 × 1.00m)

32 Shiraz Kilim 8ft 3in × 5ft 1in (2.51 × 1.55m)

33 Sine Dozar 6ft 5in × 4ft 3in (1.97 × 1.30m)

35 **Old Shiraz Soumak Bag Face** 1ft 8in x 2ft 10in (0.51 x 0.86m)

36 Old Shirvan Rug 7ft 6in x 4ft 4in (2.30 x 1.34m)

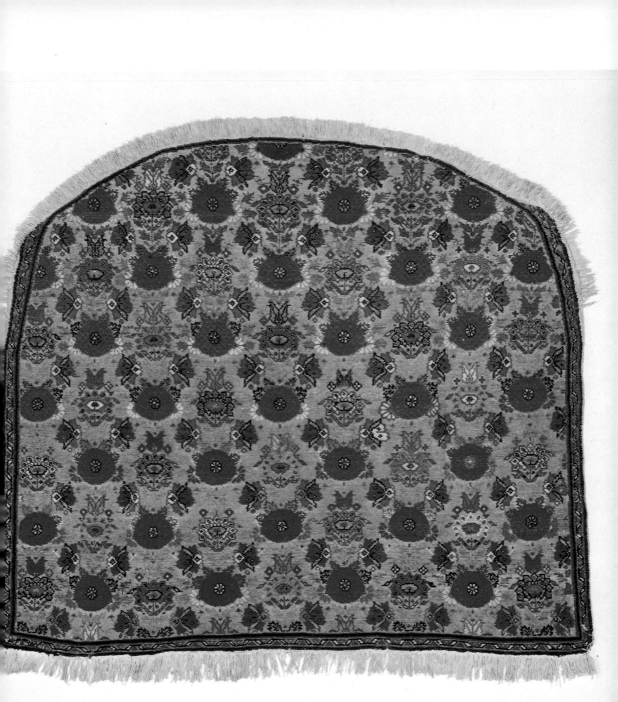

37 Fine Old Sine Saddlecloth 3ft 4in x 2ft 11in (1.02 x 0.89m)

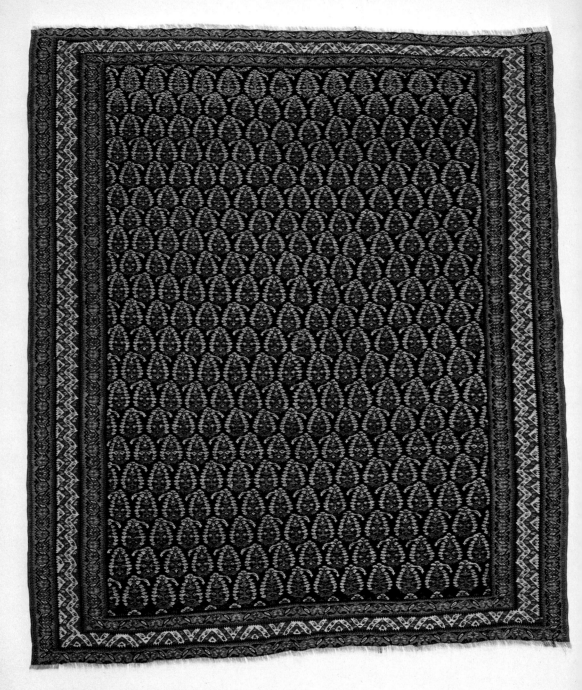

38 **Old Sine Kilim** 5ft 2in x 4ft 5in (1.57 x 1.35m)

39 Fine Old Teheran Mat 2ft 5in x 2ft 1in (0.74 x 0.64m)

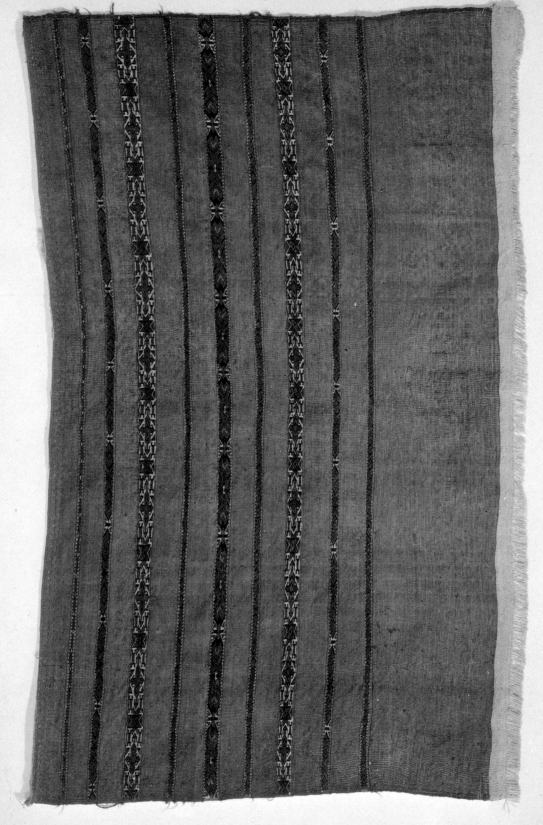

40 Old Jolam Juval 4ft 7in x 2ft 8in (1.40 x 0.81m)

41 **Afghan Rug** 4ft 4in x 2ft 9in (1.32 x 0.84m)

42 Afghan Bokara Baby 3ft 9in x 2ft 6in (1.14 x 0.76m)

43 Old Kazak Prayer Rug 5ft 3in x 2ft 8in (1.60 x 0.81m)

44 **Fine Old Kizil Ayak Hatchli** 5ft 7in x 4ft 9in (1.70 x 1.45m)

45 *(right)* **Detail of Kizil Ayak** (Plate 44)

46 **Old Shirvan Rug** 5ft x 4ft 1in (1.52 x 1.24m)

47 Hereke Dozar 6ft 11in x 4ft 7in (2.11 x 1.40m)

48 Kayseri Zaronim 4ft 5in x 2ft 9in (1.35 x 0.84m)

49 **Kurd Rug** 6ft 9in x 4ft 7in (2.06 x 1.40m)

50 Yuruk Kilim 7ft 10in x 5ft 2in (2.39 x 1.57m)

20 Antique Afghan Beshire   7ft 6in × 4ft 1in (2·30 × 1·25m)
The Beshires produce more different designs than all the other Afghan tribes put together, and probably the rarest of all are those with garden design like the piece illustrated here. Close study will show how asymmetric the designs are. In the fourth row up of small rectangles is a tree-like motif with ram's horns at the top. From there on this tree motif changes shape, and has ram's horns both at the ends and at the sides, and each of these designs is different. In fact in one of the small rectangles the weaver even managed to squeeze in nearly 1½ motifs. A fine piece with original kilim and fringe at each end. (Collection Mrs G. Izmidlian)

21 Avshar Dozar   5ft 9in × 4ft 4in (1·75 × 1·32m)
A fine specimen of a relatively new design. Although not uncommon, no two pieces are alike because of the irregularity of the motifs in the ground. This particular specimen contains an unusually high concentration of birds and animals

22 Avshar Dozar   7ft 4in × 5ft 2in (2·23 × 1·57m)
A good specimen of what is considered a typical Avshar design. Both shape and designs are irregular, but the general effect is most pleasing

23 Semi-Old Baktyar Dozar   6ft 5in × 4ft 4in (1·96 × 1·32m)
A piece 50 to 60 years old, showing tree-of-life designs up the centre, flanked by half Maj-Nun (weeping willow trees) and cypress trees on tall trunks. Note the floral motifs given to what is normally a green conifer. A design not often met these days

24 Semi-Old Russian Bokara Rug   5ft 6in × 3ft 10in (1·68 × 1·17m)
A piece about 50 years old, unusual in having a date, 1344AH (1925 AD), and signature in the main right-hand border. Note also in both borders how the small designs differ between each main motif. More often, particularly in fairly modern goods, these designs are omitted, as they involve a lot of thought and work. The guls are a little large for a piece of this size. Note the two skirts which differ in size and design

25 Semi-Old Derbend Dozar   5ft 6in × 3ft 9in (1·67 × 1·15m)
A pre-war piece dated twice 1348 AH (1929 AD), which is probably not correct. This piece shows a lot of Chinese influence in the shape of its medallion and corners. Note the irregularity of the motifs surrounding the central medallion

26 Semi-Old Ispahan Dozar   6ft 10in × 4ft 11in (2·08 × 1·50m)
A very good example of a tree-of-life design, perhaps 60 or 70 years old. As in most of these designs there is a prayer arch at the top. Note the three small birds in their nest near the top of the tree. The side panels in the border with miniature tree-of-life designs are a little unusual. The bottom and top borders are suggestive of Zille Sultan motifs

27 Semi-Old Keshan Dozar   6ft 5in × 3ft 6in (1·96 × 1·07m)
An unusual piece, carrying the crest of the government of Iraq. Probably 40 or 50 years old. Pieces like this are normally only made to special order, but its history is unknown. The border is very untypical of Keshan. Note the crests which have been repeated in the four corners. It has even been suggested that this piece was made in Iraq in the 1930's

28 Kirman Dozar   7ft 9in × 4ft 6in (2·36 × 1·37m)
This is what Kirman rugs manufactured 50 and 60 years ago looked like. There was a harmony and balance in the design, and particularly a wealth of detail, which is unfortunately lacking today. Compare with colour plate 12

29 Koum Dozar   7ft 2in × 4ft 9in (2·18 × 1·45m)
A very typical, rather elaborate prayer design Koum, manufactured in the later 1960s in a quality already getting difficult to find. Part of the design is highlighted in pure silk. Note the beautiful arrangement of flowers in the vase, made to appear almost like a peacock's tail, and also the tops of the two pillars, where the design has been copied from the capitals of the pillars at Persepolis. The border also has an unusual arched design

97

30 Moud Dozar   6ft 6in × 4ft 5in (1·98 × 1·35m)
Moud is the best of Meshed qualities, and this is an unusually elaborate design. This piece is so heavily charged with flowers that it almost merits the name Millefleurs. Although the product of the Meshed region, it has virtually nothing in common with Mesheds

31 Sarap Mossul   6ft 6in × 3ft 3in (2·00 × 1·00m)
Probably made 30/40 years ago; a type very common at that time, but today rarely seen. A very typical camel ground Sarap design. Note the small diagonal stripes in the ground and also the very wide cream outside border. It is not uncommon for Sarap strips to have plain outside borders 6–8in wide (15–20cm)

32 Shiraz Kilim   8ft 3in × 5ft 1in (2·51 × 1·55m)
A very typical Shiraz Kilim, except for the fact that many of the motifs contain reproductions of little men, rare in goods of this origin. This piece is about 30 or 35 years old, and clearly shows a lot of Abradj

33 Sine Dozar   6ft 5in × 4ft 3in (1·97 × 1·30m)
Although in immaculate condition, this piece is some 50 to 60 years old. Its design is fairly untypical of Sine rugs, and was woven on silk warp and weft

34 Carpet merchant with his stock, Shiraz Bazaar

35 Old Shiraz Soumak Bag Face   1ft 8in × 2ft 10in (0·51 × 0·86m)
There were probably two similar faces forming a normal saddle bag. Of particular interest are the different colour wools used in the warp (*vide* both fringes). The irregularity of the design gives charm to this small piece. Note the far wider left-hand border and the brocaded effect of this type of work. (Collection Mrs G. Izmidlian)

36 Old Shirvan Rug   7ft 6in × 4ft 4in (2·30 × 1·34m)
A fine specimen, possibly Seyhur, with almost full wool except that the black, particularly in the borders, suffers from corrosion. Note that this piece has 3¾ designs going up through the middle, and also the general assymmetry of the many small motifs in the ground

37 Fine Old Sine Saddlecloth   3ft 4in × 2ft 11in (1·02 × 0·89m)
Saddlecloths are rare, and pieces in this condition rarer still. These are made purely for decorative purposes and, of course, as one end has to be curved, the finish there tends to be a little ragged and the border rarely goes right round. Similar designs can be found in Kirman and Shiraz rugs. (Collection Mrs L. D. Futerman)

38 Old Sine Kilim   5ft 2in × 4ft 5in (1·57 × 1·35m)
A very fine old Sine Kilim in almost perfect condition, showing a beautiful interpretation of the Serabend or Mir design. Note the change in the size of the motifs from row to row

39 Fine Old Teheran Mat   2ft 5in × 2ft 1in (0·74 × 0·64m)
An unusual piece, with a type of millefleurs design. Note the half cypress tree at each side which is found in Haji-Hanum and Kashkai rugs. The overall effect is very reminiscent of Haji-Hanum Keshans. (One of a pair – collection Mrs G. Izmidlian)

40 Old Jolam Juval   4ft 7in × 2ft 8in (1·40 × 0·81m)
A Turkomen kilim bag face of Russian origin. Normally the whole face is piled, but occasionally such specimens are found with the piled part in narrow bands. A 60 to 70 year old piece in excellent condition, but without its back. (Private collection)

41 Afghan Rug   4ft 4in × 2ft 9in (1·32 × 0·84m)
Most modern medium-quality Afghans have a very machine-made aspect. Note the Abradj in the main border and also the toning in the ground, and particularly the introduction of an extra border on each side, all of which take it a little out of the ordinary

42 Afghan Bokara Baby   3ft 9in × 2ft 6in (1·14 × 0·76m)
A very good-quality contemporary Afghan. Many would call this a Devlet-Abad, which it

definitely is not: Devlet-Abads are far finer. Compare the sharpness of the design with Plate 41. A good specimen with ram's horns at the top of the prayer arch, but otherwise perhaps a little too regular. Note particularly the fine detail in the six borders. (Collection Mrs G. Izmidlian)

43 Old Kazak Prayer Rug   5ft 3in × 2ft 8in (1·60 × 0·81m)
A 60-year-old piece. Prayer designs in Kazaks are rare and pieces as small as this rarer still. Numerous quirks in the design. Note particularly the third 'anchor' in the main right-hand border and the double ram's horns in the middle of the first medallion where they both curve upwards, whereas in the second medallion they curve towards each other

44 Fine Old Kizil Ayak Hatchli   5ft 7in × 4ft 9in (1·70 × 1·45m)
Probably about 100 years old. A fine piece with many of the most distinctive features of the sombre-hued rugs from this area of Russia. Note the particularly long kilim and fringe which is still intact in the bottom left-hand corner. The white parts of the pile are cotton, which has of course not worn as well as the wool, giving a slightly carved appearance. Note also the zig-zag tracks on the two sides and the break in the one on the left. At the top the piece has 5½ Kibitkas or prayer arches. For a similar piece, refer to Schürmann's *Central-Asian Rugs*, pl 37. (Private collection)

45 Detail of Kizil Ayak (Plate 44): the detail in this enlargement shows the fineness of the piece. The cotton which has been used for the white is noticeable in this illustration, particularly in the top right hand corner motif

46 Old Shirvan Rug   5ft × 4ft 1in (1·52 × 1·24m)
A typical Shirvan rug. The three medallions are fairly symmetrical, but the interest really stems from all the many little different designs introduced in the ground. Unfortunately the small stars in the central medallion have run a little. Note the wine-glass border and the fact that in the side borders the glasses have bulbous stems

47 Hereke Dozar   6ft 11in × 4ft 7in (2·11 × 1·40m)
A typical modern middle-quality Hereke, with a rather machine-made aspect, but fortunately the ground colour of the medallions is not symmetrical throughout, and the medallions get larger towards the top of the rug

48 Kayseri Zaronim   4ft 5in × 2ft 9in (1·35 × 0·84m)
A typical modern Kayseri made of mercerised cotton or artificial silk. Decorative though not very hard-wearing. Similar, but coarser, pieces exist in wool

49 Kurd Rug   6ft 9in × 4ft 7in (2·06 × 1·40m)
A typical Nomadic piece probably 30 or 40 years old; called by some a Kazak Kurd because many of the motifs can also be found in the much more expensive Kazak rugs. Pieces like these are fascinating, as the designs are rarely symmetrical; this is by no means an extreme example. Close study will show how the design began with five lozenges, then a line of six lozenges, and then the design proper seems to start – but even then it is not symmetrical from side to side. For example, in the green ground of the first rectangular medallion, only three of the four corners have a type of Gul motif, and in the second large medallion similar motifs have been introduced into the green border at different places in each side. Closer study will reveal numerous other quirks and it is for these reasons that geometric pieces, and particularly nomadic ones, are so sought after

50 Yuruk Kilim   7ft 10in × 5ft 2in (2·39 × 1·57m)
A good example of a Turkish kilim from the Yuruk district. Of prayer and rather irregular design. The stepped diamond motifs in the border which contain forward and backward 'S' motifs are very irregular in colour, size and design. Note also the difference between the two end borders and the small pitchfork motif in the top dark blue border. Further study will reveal many other interesting quirks

Appendix (i) Qualities of Carpets

A bewildering variety of names is used to describe the many different types of oriental carpets – what are technically known as their Qualities. Usually the name of the region or village with which the carpet's manufacture first became associated is used, or it may be the name of the tribe who made it; the name may, however, refer additionally to a method of fabrication, eg kilim; or to the type of pattern, eg hunting carpet; or to the use for which it was designed, eg prayer rug.

An experienced carpet dealer or collector will be able to identify a carpet by a whole range of signs: the pattern, the material it is made from, the closeness and type of knotting, the signs of age, and so on. By putting these indicators together he will identify a Keshan carpet, a Shiraz rug, a Saff prayer rug, and so on. This skill can only come from years of experience, and there are books much more detailed than this one which will help you to identify the different varieties. It is quite unnecessary to be able to make these identifications in order to appreciate the beauty of oriental carpets, but the more rugs and carpets one sees, and the more one is able to talk about them with well-informed dealers and collectors, the easier it will become to recognise the main types, and the deeper one's appreciation will grow. As a start, here is a list that describes the most important of these Qualities.

The spelling of place names has always presented difficulties, as they have to be transliterated into roman characters and wide differences occur between different authorities. It will be found that a g or a k is often inserted in front of an h, or an h after a g, so as to make the sound a little more guttural. Arabic is a very guttural-sounding language. We have, in principle, adhered to one consistent spelling throughout this book, which are the forms that have been used in the author's firm for many years, but alternative spellings for some terms are given in this list.

Names printed in SMALL CAPITALS indicate that there is an entry in this list under that name. Plate references after an entry refer to the illustrations between pages 48 and 97. All the terms for sizes, types of weave and designs are described in the Glossary, which follows this list of Qualities.

Abade (Persian), a village south of Ispahan. Carpet making has been established here only in recent years; the most common pattern is a single diamond shape in the middle of the field, surrounded by small geometrical shapes; it looks like a factory-made SHIRAZ but on a cotton warp and weft. Another less common pattern consists of a vase of roses repeated to cover the entire field, known as the zilli-sultan motif.

Afghan (Afghan), the general term for all rugs and carpets from Afghanistan. They can be recognised fairly easily from their typical pattern, which consists of rows of octagonal guls, often separated by stylized branches of trees. The basic colour is a strong red, with a very dark blue that is almost black. Yellow is sometimes found in pieces from the BESHIRE region and the usual gul is replaced by a VERAMIN type of rose pattern about the size of a BOKARA gul. (Plates 19, 20, 41 and 42).

Afghan Bokara (Afghan), an AFGHAN rug with a BOKARA design (Plate 42).

Afshar, see AVSHAR.

Ahar (Persian), a village famous for its carpets, similar to those of HERIZ, but with curvilinear rather than the Heriz's geometric designs.

Anatole (Turkish), a general term covering rugs from GIORDES, KAYSERI, LADIK, MELAS and some other Turkish districts.

Arasbaran (Persian), a type of HAMADAN carpet, similar to the KARAJA. The design often incorporates two or three large geometric medallions, which almost touch and cover nearly the whole ground. They are more common in carpet than in rug sizes.

Ardebil see ERDEBIL.

Avshar (Persian), nomadic tribe that has settled near Kirman. The rugs are brightly coloured in red and blue and ivory; a variety of designs are used, some with large lozenges, some with boteh, but mainly geometric patterns based on a design of usually two but sometimes three or more large diamond-shaped medallions filled with and surrounded by a mass of small motifs (Plates 1, 21 and 22). The warp threads tend to be much thicker than the weft threads, giving the back of the rug a ribbed appearance.

Baktyar (Persian), a tribe inhabiting an area that contains hundreds of villages. The typical pattern consists of rows of squares or guls entirely filling the field; the guls are filled with stylized floral designs, which may be repeated a number of times in each carpet (Plates 2 and 23). The quality of some pieces from this area was at one time not good, use being made of wool from the backs of dead sheep, but there has been a revival in the past quarter century. See BIBIBAFF, CHELESHOTOR, and HINIKHAN.

Baluchi, see BELOUDJ

Begardeh (Persian), a type of HAMADAN, usually of excellent quality, not dissimilar to a good HUSSEINABAD, but rather thicker and with a crenellated effect in the medallion and corners (Plate 6).

Beloudj (Persian, Afghan), carpets and rugs made by nomadic tribes who used to trek across what is now the Iranian/Afghanistan border. These rugs are not made in Baluchistan, a group of states in Pakistan, as some spellings of the name would suggest. Many of the pieces are prayer rugs, with red and dark blue predominant, and the colouring is similar to that of AFGHANS, but the BELOUDJ are of finer stitch (Plate 4). As the nomad tribes have settled, the rugs made in Persia, called MESHED-BELOUDJ (as they are marketed in the town of Meshed), have tended to develop rather differently to those made in Afghanistan, called HERAT-BELOUDJ (as they are marketed in Herat, the next large town on the main trade route east after leaving Meshed).

The Meshed-Beloudj are now made mainly on cotton warps and wefts, and are generally of better design and quality, and more regular in workmanship than the Herat-Beloudj, but they are now tending to become a little stereotyped as the nomads settle. The design is normally a small all-over pattern in geometric form.

The Herat-Beloudj, on the other hand, are still made with wool warp and weft, sometimes mixed with goat or camel hair; most of them are far cheaper than the Meshed-Beloudj, but the best and finest old Beloudj pieces are Herat, not Meshed.

The Meshed-Beloudj are very hard wearing; they have fewer prayer designs than the Herat-Beloudj. The Herat-Beloudj often have very finely woven kilims at each end, but their work is pulled up so tightly that it gives the rug a barrel shape, with wrinkles due to the kilim pulling.

Beloudj Bokara (Persian), a BELOUDJ with BOKARA design.

Beloutchi, see BELOUDJ

Beludsh, see BELOUDJ

Bergamo (Turkish), town north of Izmir producing mainly rugs and carpets up to about 9ft by 6ft. The designs are geometric, usually with one or more large medallions surrounded by small motifs. The colours are deep red and dark blue, with the blue of old pieces often worn down to the warp and weft due to poor dyes, giving an embossed effect.

Beschir, see BESHIRE

Beshire (Afghan), a tribe that has settled on the borders of Turkmenistan, Uzbekistan and Afghanistan. Their carpets are now traded from Kabul. The designs are often floral patterns freely executed, and the predominant colours are red, dark blue and always, though sometimes very little, yellow (Plate 20).

Bibibaff (Persian), one of the better qualites of BAKTYAR carpet, said to be named after the princess Bibi-Hanum, the wife of a local chieftain, who inspired a revival in these carpets about a quarter of a century ago.

Bidjar (Persian), town in Kurdistan. The carpets made here are very heavy and stiff and have an exceptionally thick pile, due to the use of an unusually large number of weft threads which are beaten down with a thicker iron comb than is usual elsewhere. The colouring is often very fine and the patterns make much use of the herati design, but often have borders with roses (known as French design) which bear no relation at all to the rest.

Bijar, see BIDJAR

Birjand (Persian), a good quality MESHED.

Bokara (Russian), name for the rugs produced by the TURKOMEN tribes and for the design associated with these rugs. The typical pattern consists of several rows of guls, often linked by lines running from top to bottom and from side to side of the carpet; these lines intersect in the centre of each gul, dividing it into two pairs of alternately patterned and coloured segments; a cross-shaped motif fills the spaces between the rows of guls (Plate 24). These pieces can sometimes be found with a skirt at each end. Rugs with Bokara designs are now produced in several places, and differ greatly among themselves. Those made in Persia are called YAMOUT and BELOUDJ; the YAMOUT tends to be in very sharp red, the BELOUDJ in a very dull red, almost burgundy. Those made in Pakistan, known as PAKISTAN BOKARA, come in all colours from deep chocolate brown to cream and a full range of pastel tones – which are utterly out of keeping with the Bokara tradition. The wool and knots differ also. The AFGHAN BOKARA (Plate 42) is the coarsest but as production in Russia is becoming so standardised today it retains most character and is probably to be classed as equal with BELOUDJ BOKARA as the most desirable in the range; the RUSSIAN BOKARA should be placed third, the YAMOUT fourth and the PAKISTAN last. And yet the new Russian is still the most sought after, though the old ones come out on top.

Borchalou (Persian), one of the finer knotted types of rug from the HAMADAN region. The designs are generally highly floral, similar to KIRMANS, and have medallions on covered red or cream ground. Production is today mainly of high-quality rugs, but poor dyes are now often used so they have a tendency to run.

Bukhara, see BOKARA

Caucasus (Russian), area producing a distinct group of rugs and carpets on the border between Persia and Russia. The main districts are KAZAK, SHIRVAN, DERBEND, KARABAGH and ERIVAN. These are subdivided into towns, but the differences between towns is small and difficult to demonstrate. In general, Caucasian carpets have strictly geometric designs and are marked by a primitive vigour that is greatly admired today (Plates 25, 36, 43 and 46). In certain places, however, Armenian weavers produced carpets with mainly floral designs, and these are found at KARABAGH and ERIVAN.

Cheleshotor (Persian), the finest kind of BAKTYAR. The design usually has a medallion surrounded by multi-coloured rosettes.

Chi-chi (Russian), a type of SHIRVAN rug.

Dagestan (Russian), alternative name for the Caucasian DERBEND carpets.

Devlet-Abad (Afghan), the best type of AFGHAN. It is very rarely seen, and the name is now commonly applied to poorer qualities in order to enhance them. The backs usually have a pink appearance.

Derbend (Russian), town in the CAUCASUS whose carpets resemble SHIRVANS but are coarser. The colouring is basically red with blue or cream, often in floral designs (Plate 25).

Djoshegan, see JOSHAGHAN

Dorosch (Persian), hills near MESHED in Khorassan. The herati design originated from this area. These carpets can be identified by studying their backs; the weft is normally a single thread of yarn but every eight or nine rows it is composed of three threads which show up clearly.

Egyptian (Egyptian), there has been a small production of rugs mainly in Keshan design and many in pure silk, starting in the 1970s. Quality and stitch are good, but the wool is a little soft. In a few years time they may prove difficult to distinguish from the real thing.

Erdebil (Persian), an area in the north-west of Iran, producing carpets with Caucasian designs similar to SHIRVAN. This is also the centre for marketing strips made in the surrounding villages and known as Erdebil runners.

Erivan (Russian), town in the CAUCASUS and capital of Armenia. The rugs made here, mostly by Armenians and Tartars are marked by a brownish tinge in the red, probably caused by the nature of the local water, and are mainly of floral designs though some are similar to KAZAKS.

Ersari (Afghan), a TURKOMEN tribe producing a type of AFGHAN rug.

Ezineh (Turkish), a similar rug to BERGAMO but coarser.

Feraghan (Persian), a district once famous for its producton of carpets and rugs, but now of less importance (Plate 5). It has, however, given its name to a distinctive variant of the herati pattern; See Glossary.

Gashgai, see KASHKAI

Gendje (Russian), a Caucasian rug similar to KAZAK, often with a Barber's Pole design in the ground.

Ghoum, see KOUM

Giordes (Turkish), fine old rugs, generally in prayer design and nearly always with a plain ground. They had one wide border with one or more guard stripes on each side. The modern production can be very coarse and of poor colour. This is also the name of the Turkish knot. See Glossary.

Gorovan (Persian), a cheaper quality of HERIZ.

Hamadan (Persian), city in Kurdistan and the centre of the largest carpet producing area in the world. The sheep of this district provide what is probably the hardest-wearing wool used anywhere for the manufacture of carpets (Plate 6). There is today an increasing amount of factory production but the output is still predominantly from a cottage industry; because of this rugs must outnumber carpets perhaps fifty to one and the quality tends to be a little on the coarse side. As the bulk of the output is not organised, a wider variety of designs can be found than from almost any other district; patterns are equally divided between those with all-over designs and those with medallions; very few medallion pieces have open grounds. The most common design is the Sine or Feraghan, which is often used on pieces with all-over designs and to fill the ground of pieces with medallions. This design, however, is interpreted in so many different ways that it is often only recognisable by an expert, and pieces using it may look quite dissimilar just as the variety of medallions and borders is endless. The predominant ground colour is red, but blue is also common.

Many of the outlying villages have given their names to special designs which they originated and still use (though they may be used in other places as well), and other names have been given to specific designs which have no real place of origin. The most important of these are ARASBARAN, BOR-CHALOU, FERAGHAN, HUSSEINABAD, INDJI-LAS, JOZAN, KAPUTRENK, KARAJA, KURD, LEYLAHAN, MAHAL, MAZLAGAN, MELAYIR, MIANEH, SAVEH, SHAHSEVEN, SHARIBAFF, TAFRISH, TUSERKHAN, WEISZ.

Haroun (Persian), a type of KESHAN carpet of poor wool less carefully knotted than is usual with carpets from this area, and priced much lower. The pattern is indistinct at the back, and the weft threads show up irregularly.

Herat-Beloudj (Afghan), type of BELOUDJ rug marketed through the town of Herat on the trade route to the east. (See Beloudj).

Hereke (Turkish), among the finest rugs made anywhere. They were generally of Persian design, of good wool and also of silk with gold and silver metallic thread, in soft pastel colours. Old examples are very expensive; modern work ranges from very fine to very ordinary (Plate 47).

Heriz (Persian), town near TABRIZ and the centre of an important carpet industry. The patterns tend to be angular, introducing a large central medallion and prominent corner pieces, in warm, soft colours (Plate 7). They are very hard wearing with good colours; cheaper qualities are GOROVAN and MEHRABAN. Old Heriz can be found in pure silk in rug and carpet sizes, very finely knotted but quite different from the coarse but very hard wearing woollen production.

Hinikhan (Persian), a poorish BAKTYAR, thin, coarse and mainly in Kellay sizes.

Husseinabad (Persian), a finer type of HAMADAN carpet or rug.

Indjilas (Persian), a type of HAMADAN rug, once extensively made but now less commonly seen. They are of fine quality, similar to the FERAGHAN in appearance.

Indo-Persian (Indian), now used to denote coarse to middle quality modern rugs mainly of Persian design. There are two main types. JAIPUR is better and heavier than AGRA production where thinner and cheaper goods are produced.

Isfahan, see ISPAHAN

Ispahan (Persian), ancient capital of Persia and one of its most historic cities. A flourishing carpet industry was re-established here during the reign of Shah Abbas (1586–1628) and some of the finest carpets of the period were made here. After capture by the Afghans and the disappearance of the Persian court, carpet making declined but has been revived during this century. The typical design is a central medallion surrounded by interlacing tendrils that entirely fill the field; there may sometimes be corner pieces that reflect the flowing, floral character of the whole pattern (Plates 8 and 26). Today much silk is used in the designs and they are the finest of modern Persian production after NAYIN. To make these very fine pieces expert craftsmen are needed but they have to work from very exact cartoons and are allowed no 'poetic licence'; so although the final result is very fine they tend to look machine-made and characterless and the modern ones surprisingly rarely become silky, even after heavy wear.

Isparta, see SPARTA

Jaipur (Indian), the name given to heavy, better quality Indo-Persians. Pure silk rugs are now being woven.

Jaldar (Pakistan), the name now given to many of the rugs woven in the Karachi district, mainly of non-Bokara designs.

Jarkand, see YARKAND

Joshaghan (Persian), village in central Iran. The typical design of its carpets is based on a diamond-shaped pattern (see Glossary). Corner pieces may be outlined by a Greek key pattern. These shapes will often be edged with white, thus making them stand out clearly. These carpets are often of poor quality but the better ones are known as MOUCHAKAR and MEY-MEY, although modern pieces bear almost no relation to the old.

Kansu (Chinese), a carpet somewhat similar to SAMARKAND but with more Chinese characteristics.

Jozan (Persian), a very thick, heavy rug from the HAMADAN area. The production is mostly of high quality rugs, which are similar to SAROUKS and are often sold as such.

Kaputrenk (Persian), probably the least attractive of any of the carpets from the HAMADAN area; the wool used is possibly the worst in the district. This, nevertheless, is a relative judgement and the wool is far better than that from almost all other lands. Kaputrenks are heavier than most other HAMADANS, and in the middle price range.

Karabagh (Russian), region of the CAUCASUS largely inhabited by Armenians. It produced rugs with rich colours and a wide range of designs. Some of the designs are based on Persian patterns, with herati, boteh and medallion motifs; some are based on French Savonnerie originals.

Karachi (Pakistan), the origin of many Pakistan rugs and carpets of non-Bokara (Jaldar) designs.

Karaja (Persian), an area meaning 'black mountain' on the frontier between Iran and the USSR. The designs are similar to those of the CAUCASUS, but very much coarser and of worse wool. It is the centre of production of cheap rugs and carpets but the few good ones are excellent. Again, modern production looks very different from the old.

Kasak, see KAZAK

Kashan, see KESHAN

Kashgar (Chinese), a carpet from Chinese Turkestan similar to SAMARKAND.

Kashkai (Persian), tribe inhabiting the area of the Fars upland (Shiraz area). Their carpets are similar to those of SHIRAZ, but are noted for their superior wool and finer knotting and are probably the finest of this district. The typical design introduces one or more diamond-shaped lozenges on a field scattered with floral motifs. Many of the rugs from the district with prayer designs are Kashkai.

Kashmir (Indian), in north-west India, is a source of fine to very fine rugs of Persian designs made of good wool or wool and silk. NB The so-called 'Kashmir' wool of which most Pakistan carpets are made is not as hard wearing.

Kayseri (Turkish), many pieces of prayer design, though as with many other Turkish qualities, Persian designs are also copied. The wool used is rather low grade and many not very old pieces are now quite worn out (Plate 48). Some silk rugs are produced, but today many are made of artificial silk (mercerised cotton) which gives a silky looking but poor wearing result. Most 'family prayer rugs', called SAFFS, come from Kayseri, though a few are to be found from SAMARKAND.

Kazak (Russian), area in the southern CAUCASUS. The rugs from here are noted for their good quality wool, deep pile, and strong primitive designs (Plate 43). These are of coarse stitch, basically geometrical, strongly angular and brightly coloured. The top and bottom ends are usually finished with narrow kilims.

Kerman, see KIRMAN

Keshan (Persian), town in central Iran. It was famous in the sixteenth century for its silk carpets depicting hunting scenes, of which a superb example is the Vienna hunting carpet of the House of Hapsburg. Metal brocading was sometimes woven into these carpets and in their detail they almost attained the delicacy of a painting. Carpet making here was interrupted by the Afghan invasion in 1722, but was revived towards the end of the nineteenth century. These examples are noted for their fine knotting and good quality wool and are known as Keshan Moctashemi. The tradition of picture designs has, to some extent, been maintained but a more typical design introduces a large central medallion, corner pieces that reflect the same pattern, and intertwined flowers and tendrils spreading over the field. Of all the regions that produce pieces with fine knotting Keshan is the one with by far the best and silkiest wool. Old silk pieces are attractive and command a high price, but today's small production of pure silk rugs and carpets is of poorish quality (Plates 9, 10 and 27).

Kherkin (Afghan), term for a type of AFGHAN carpet made by Turkomen nomads. Their wool is lustrous and their design is based on simple guls. Because of their coarse stitch, this is almost the worst quality of Afghan.

Khorassan (Persian), an alternative term for the carpets of MESHED, though generally much finer and rarely seen today.

Kirman (Persian), city in an arid area of south-east Iran, near the beautiful mausoleum of Shah Nimatullah. The carpets are in elaborate floral designs, usually with central medallions but sometimes with the intricate pattern over the entire field. Some carpets carry a Korani pattern, derived from the bookbindings of the Koran. The production today is almost exclusively from factories, and hence rather lacking individual character; some of the carpets tend to be designed more with an eye to European taste than to authentic Persian tradition, taking their patterns from French Aubussons. The wool is generally rather soft, and so not very hard wearing (Plates 12 and 28).

Older Kirmans were made with a short pile, but in recent years, as with SAROUKS, there has been a tendency to give them thicker piles as this was preferred for the American market. These thick Kirmans, particularly those with a medallion on open cream, beige or white grounds are known as 'American Kirmans'.

Buyers should beware of pieces – which are the majority – with open plain grounds, that is a single colour over most of the field. Such grounds frequently have fewer stitches than in the borders and medallion. To check, the carpet should be folded so that one can feel the double thickness of both the border and the ground side by side. They should feel exactly the same thickness; if they don't, the purchase should be avoided.

Kirscheyir (Turkish), normally geometric rugs with a central medallion on a covered ground. These rugs often have an extra border at the top and bottom, and are sometimes called, inaccurately, 'double-ended' prayer rugs. The colouring is mainly red.

Kizil Ayak (Russian and Afghan), type of PENDIK rug, usually very fine. There is virtually no modern production, though the name is often given to inferior qualities (Plate 44).

Konya (Turkish), type of coarse rug with geometric design, often in crude colours, especially today. The wool is of poor quality. Because of their strong colours many examples have been gold washed. Many prayer designs are employed, sometimes with a large head or tablet above the mehrab.

Kotan (Chinese), a carpet from Chinese Turkestan similar to SAMARKAND.

Koum (Persian), city famous for its shrine of Fatimah and the golden cupola of its mosque. Carpet making was not started here until 1930, but since that date an excellent reputation has been built up, with a fine weave and well-conceived patterns introducing the boteh, the zilli-sultan, the KESHAN central medallion, figurals, hunting designs, and other classic features. The colouring was often vivid and the central ground in white or ivory but is now often in more pastel shades. There are no original designs – only copies of other's motifs (Plates 13 and 29). The carpets are mainly of good quality, but some are poor. Silk Koums made today are better than silk KESHANS.

Kuba (Russian), an important centre for carpet making in the SHIRVAN district. It was noted for its so-called 'dragon carpets'. See Glossary.

Kum-Kapu (Turkish), early twentieth century workshop in Istanbul producing very good imitations of antique carpets of exceptional fineness.

Kurd (Persian and Turkish), carpets woven by nomads in Kurdistan which is on the Persian-Turkish frontier. Those made in Persia belong to the Hamadan group, but those woven in Turkey are very Turkish in appearance. In quality and texture they all resemble poor Kazaks, the Turkish more so than the Persian. Their nomadic geometric designs are very different and are among the most irregular produced. The weave is fairly coarse and the output consists mainly of larger than average Dozar sizes in the middle price range (Plate 49).

Ladik (Turkish), rugs of good wool, usually in prayer design and often with large 'heads' (as with KONYA). Three or more tulips usually spring from the top of the mehrab. Colouring is red or dark blue. Old examples are much sought after.

Lahore (Pakistan), low to middle quality rugs mainly of Bokara design.

Laver (Persian), a top quality KIRMAN, not now made (Plate 11).

Leylahan (Persian), a HAMADAN type rug, almost invariably with a light red or pink ground. The design is usually large bunches of small flowers in an all-over pattern, but there is sometimes a small medallion in the middle. The quality is fairly fine.

Lilihan, see LEYLAHAN

Luristan (Persian), area in south-west Iran inhabited by the Luri tribes. Their rugs are similar to KURDS, brightly coloured in simple geometric designs.

Maden (Turkish), a common quality similar to KONYA. Some years ago it was regarded as inferior, but today is better as the colours are not so hard.

Mahal (Persian), type of carpet produced in the HAMADAN area with soft silky wool and large knots. Tabachi (wool from dead sheep) is sometimes used, and the general quality is indifferent.

Makhmalbaff (Persian), good quality MESHED carpet, made of good, lustrous wool.

Malayer, see MELAYIR.

Mazlagan (Persian), a type of rug from a village near HAMADAN. The design is distinctive, consisting of a large serrated central medallion whose surrounding field is edged with a pair of zig-zag lines stretching the length of the carpet. The border is usually in three bands. Motifs of rosettes are freely used for decoration. Production is mainly of rugs, which vary in quality from low to high priced.

Mecca Shiraz (Persian), after KASHKAI the second finest carpet from the SHIRAZ region (Plate 15).

Mehraban (Persian), village producing HERIZ type carpets, generally in all-over designs in lower quality.

Melas (Turkish), prayer rugs of good wool, similar to GIORDES and LADIK. They often have very attractive light brown grounds and golden borders. Old examples are much sought after but it is doubtful if any are made today.

Melayir (Persian), a HAMADAN district rug with a fine reputation, resembling a cross between a BORCHALOU and a LEYLAHAN. The pile is generally thick and the ground colour blue, covered with fairly large all-over floral designs. Production today has almost ceased, but old examples are most attractive, in fact most *fine* old Hamadans are really Melayirs but the range of designs was greater and quite different from the floral designs of more recent production. The best are often misnamed SINE, or SINE-HAMADAN or even SAROUK.

Meshed (Persian), capital of Khorassan and a holy city to the Shiites, the centre of a large carpet making district. The wool is exceptionally soft. Two types of carpet are produced, one using the Persian and the other the Turkish knot, but both employ similar patterns, which are floral and in brilliant colours, often with very sharp orange and with a red that is almost mauve. The cheaper qualities are not very hard wearing, but the better ones known as BIRJAND, DOROSCH, MAKHMALBAFF and MOUD can be very long lasting, Moud being the finest and Makhmalbaff the silkiest.

Meshed-Beloudj (Persian), type of BELOUDJ rug marketed through the town of Meshed (Plate 4).

Mey-Mey (Persian), good quality JOSHAGHAN carpet, similar to MOUCHAKAR (a term best known in Germany).

Mianeh (Persian), a type of ARASBARAN carpet.

Milas, see MELAS

Mir (Persian), type of carpet carrying a design of small botehs. The name is often given to good quality SERABEND carpets. See Glossary.

Mori (Afghan), very fine and thin rugs, usually of BOKARA or Hatchli design, of recent manufacture. They can unfortunately fairly easily be confused with Russian Bokaras and Hatchlis.

Mossul (Persian), term applied inaccurately, to Kurdish carpets from the HAMADAN area. At one time these carpets were traded through Mossul. Now the name is used to describe a size of rug. See Glossary.

Mouchakar (Persian), small village producing carpets similar to those of JOSHAGAN, but much finer (Plate 16).

Moud (Persian), the finest type of MESHED carpet (Plate 30).

Mushkebad (Persian), town near Sultanabad (now Arak) whose name has been appropriated to describe the poorest quality MAHAL carpets.

Nain, see NAYIN

Nayin (Persian), town near ISPAHAN, and producing carpets of similar design. The colours tend to be pale, with cool shades of blue or green set off by ivory or beige. These are the finest of all modern Persians, but the general comments on ISPAHAN apply also to Nayin.

Ningsia (Chinese), a carpet similar to KANSU.

Oushak (Turkish), the original 'Holbein' carpet and the ubiquitous 'Turkey' carpet of pre-war days. They were very hard wearing, although coarse, and mainly in all-over designs in green, red and dark blue. Few rugs were produced but carpets were made in all shapes and sizes, including Kellays and Strips. The designs are in some ways reminiscent of HERIZ, but with large bold stars.

Pakistan (Pakistan), rugs and carpets are sometimes finely knotted but more frequently are made of the very poorest wool and suffer from the lack of originality inseparable from derivative work. They become limp with use and are normally not very hard wearing. Those made in LAHORE are mainly of BOKARA designs and are cheaper than those known as KARACHI quality which are made mainly in the surrounding towns. The latter are of better quality and largely of JALDAR designs which are adapted from and often a mixture of Bokara, Yamout and Caucasian designs.

Panderma (Turkish), prayer rugs, often of poor wool or poor art silk. Their knotting is fairly fine. They are easily distinguished by the large number of equal width borders. They wear very badly, perhaps because of poor dyes that damage the wool.

Pendik (Russian and Afghan), a fortified oasis south of Merv, and the name applied to a range of carpets made by TURKOMEN tribes:

(1) A type whose main design is based on stepped guls. The older examples are very finely knotted and are usually in red and blue (Plate 19). More recent examples are less densely knotted, with longer pile and in a brownish-red, sometimes even chocolate-brown.

(2) A type known as KIZIL-AYAK (golden foot) is of fine quality and is marked by the contrast between the basic brownish-red colouring and a sharp white produced by the use of cotton instead of wool for some

of the white knots. Among the smaller Sedjadé sizes is the engsi (a rug originally used as a door flap for tent entrances) which has an unique hatchli design. The arms of the hatchli (cross) and the field between them, are all elaborately decorated. Below the hatchli there is a band of rectangles, and incorporated in the top border is a row of mehrabs. The bottom border or skirt is very wide and carries a reddish-brown or gold band, hence its name. The side borders are also unusually wide, whilst the top border is very narrow, and the top fringe is invariably turned under and sewn back so that it cannot be seen. The Russian Pendiks and Hatchlis (Plate 44) are fine, the Afghan ones coarser but generally of good wool.

Pergama, see BERGAMO

Pesch-Meshed (Persian), literally 'wool from Meshed', the name given to the finest carpets from HERIZ. (This term is best known in Germany.)

Pinde, see PENDIK

Qashgai, see KASHKAI

Qum, see KOUM

Ravar, see LAVER

Royal, a prefix to BOKARA, KIRMAN, TABRIZ and some other qualities, applied by retailers mainly to make a piece seem more desirable and so justify a higher price.

Russian Bokara (Russian), the original type of BOKARA carpet, as made by the TEKKE tribe in the area of Merv (Plate 24). It is sometimes called Real Bokara.

Saff (Turkish), type of family prayer rug made in KAYSERI. It contains six to ten mehrabs arranged down the length of the rug, so that several people may kneel side by side, though in fact the space allowed is usually inadequate for this actually to happen. It is frequently made of art silk, so is not hard wearing and more decorative than practical.

Salor (Afghan), a TURKOMEN tribe producing AFGHAN rugs with a distinct variant of gul motif and of excellent quality.

Samarkand (Chinese), Russian city that has acted as the main trading centre for the sale of carpets from Chinese Turkestan to the West. For this reason, the wholly incorrect name of Samarkand has become attached to the carpets produced by nomads in the west of China. The quality of the wool and work is poor but their designs are very beautiful and much sought after. A typical motif is a flowering pomegranate tree growing from a vase at each end with branches spreading over the entire field. Decorations of the field are typically rounded, while those of the borders are geometric, often featuring the Greek key pattern.

Saph, see SAFF

Sarap (Persian), an area near ERDEBIL producing rugs and strips noted for the excellence of their wool. The designs are similar to those of HERIZ, but the predominating colour is camel (Plate 31).

Sarouk (Persian), a village near Arak which gives its name to carpets from the surrounding area. The quality is fine and the design is distinctive; it introduces a large central medallion, basically composed of floral motifs; the borders are simpler than in most Persian carpets, consisting of just one broad border with a narrow one on each side (Plates 17 and 18). Recent design, as with those of KIRMAN, shows signs of Western influence. The pile, too, has undergone a change. Older Sarouks, as well as KIRMANS, before World War I, were made with a pile as short as KESHANS, but – largely due to the wish to cater for the American market – thick pieces with a long pile are now most common; these are sometimes known as American Sarouks.

Sarouk Mahal (Persian), one of the best kinds of MAHAL carpet.

Saruq, see SAROUK

Saveh (Persian), a type of HUSSEINABAD of which production has recently restarted. But whereas the HUSSEINABAD often features a Feraghan design these frequently copy the designs of MELAYIR or of SAMARKAND carpets. Most pieces are Zaronim size rugs in the middle price group, rather coarse and of poor colours.

Sechur, see SEYHUR

Sehna, see SINE

Senne, see SINE

Serabend (Persian), mountainous area in Central Persia producing carpets with a distinctive design of rows of small botehs, from which the Paisley design is derived (see Glossary). The finest carpets of this kind are the MIR but these are now being widely copied in India.

Seyhur (Russian), a type of SHIRVAN rug, usually with a large St Andrews type cross as design and a distinctive blue and white running dog border.

Shahseven (Persian), a type of HAMADAN rug whose production has been fairly recent. Shahsevens were one time brigands who roamed the TABRIZ area. The variety of geometric designs unfortunately defies description, although many have a SAMARKAND influence. The production is of good middle quality rugs at relatively inexpensive prices.

Sharibaff (Persian), one of the finest and certainly the rarest of the carpets produced in the HAMADAN district. It is almost indistinguishable in appearance from a SAROUK, but is considerably finer in knotting and is stiffer, rather like a BIDJAR. The design is usually a medallion on a covered cream ground. These rank with the most expensive of Persian carpets, like KESHAN, KIRMAN, KOUM and TABRIZ.

Shiraz (Persian), capital of the Fars province and trading centre for the rugs made by the nomads of the surrounding area. Most of these are still made on ground looms from wool dyed with vegetable dyes. The most distinctive design introduces one or more diamond-shaped lozenges as the predominant feature in the field; the narrow border often contains a row of diagonal stripes. The majority of Persian Kilims come from this area. (See also MECCA SHIRAZ, KASHKAI and ABADE). (Plates 32 and 35).

Shirvan (Russian), district in the CAUCASUS and the centre of a long-established carpet industry. The designs vary greatly but, like all designs from this area, are basically geometrical. In the south of the Caucasus the ends of the warp threads at the bottom of the carpet are left as loops, but in the north Caucasus they are cut and knotted at the bottom as well as at the top. These are the finest of Russians, but subdivided by the connoisseur (Plates 36 and 46).

Sine (Persian) (pronounced Siné) capital of Kurdistan. The rugs made here are, however, quite different from those made in the Kurdish villages. They are very finely knotted, in fact almost the finest stitch of any Persian carpets; the weave is such that if the back is rubbed with one's knuckles it feels as rough as sandpaper. Their designs are based on the herati and the boteh, which are often used in all-over patterns, but some introduce a central medallion. This town also produces the finest of kilims (Plates 33, 37 and 38).

Sine-Hamadan (Persian), inaccurate term for a MELAYIR rug.

Sivas (Turkish), rugs and carpets factory-produced up to fairly large sizes. They usually look like Persians and are quite good copies of TABRIZ designs but they can be identified from their backs which show such a regular Turkish knot that they almost look machine made. They are finely knotted from good wool. There is a blueish tinge to their colours but often a cream ground, as they were made largely for Western taste.

Soumak (Russian, Persian, Turkish), a town in the CAUCASUS which has given its name to a type of woven carpet originally produced in Dagestan. The designs are Caucasian in style, geometric, and often featuring diamond-shaped lozenges in blue on a dull red field. Rugs in Soumak weave are also produced in Persia and Turkey (Plate 35).

Sparta (Turkish), similar but coarser type of production to SIVAS, in all sizes up to some very large carpets. In addition to Persian, Chinese designs are also sometimes copied.

Suleymani (Afghan), a good middle-quality AFGHAN.

Sumak, see SOUMAK

Tabriz (Persian), important and historic city in north-west Iran, housing a number of carpet factories, established since the middle of the nineteenth century. Some of these contain large looms capable of producing carpets up to 35ft wide. The designs incorporate all the classical motifs of Persian carpets, often introducing a large central medallion with free floral decorations surrounding it. With such a large output, the quality of Tabriz carpets can vary from very fine to very poor. It is renowned for its Hunting design carpets; and for the animal faces sometimes cleverly worked into the flowers of the patterns. See border illustrated on page 122 and note the four deers' heads in the left hand motif and the rather puzzled lion's face in the middle of the right hand flower. Old TABRIZ rugs and carpets in pure silk are similar to the old HERIZ silks, and are equally expensive.

Tafrish (Persian), a good quality rug from the HAMADAN area.

Talish (Russian), area producing rugs with a thick pile, some of which are of KAZAK and some of SHIRVAN characteristics.

Tebriz, see TABRIZ

Teheran (Persian), modern capital of Iran. This city does not possess a long carpet making tradition but during this century a hand-loom factory has been set up under the patronage of the Shah to produce carpets of the finest quality. The standard of workmanship is very high. The designs are all copies from classical Persian pieces (Plate 39).

Tekke (Afghan), a Turkomen tribe producing excellent BOKARA type rugs.

Tibet (Indian), a limited production by Tibetan refugees in India of rugs that look like coarse, primitive Chinese.

Turkomen (Afghan, Persian and Russian), the name applied to carpets woven by nomad tribes of Turkish origin, who lived in Russian Turkestan, Iran and Afghanistan. They constitute one of the most important groups of nomad-style carpets, and are generally to be recognised by their dark red colouring. The pattern is geometrical, often based upon rows of guls. Among the most important types are BOKARA, YAMOUT, BESHIRE, PENDIK, AFGHAN and BELOUDJ.

Tuzerkhan (Persian), rug of the HAMADAN district. It invariably consists of a medallion on a large plain camel-coloured ground; the colouring is in bright reds and greens.

Ushak, see OUSHAK

Veramin (Persian), town south of Teheran

producing fine carpets often with mina-khani design of a field scattered with a regular pattern of small flowers. Sometimes the zilli-sultan, vase of flowers, design is used in the larger sizes. Simpler, village-style rugs are also produced here, as well as kilims.

Weisz (Persian), a rug from the HAMADAN district. It is very hard and stiff, similar to a BIDJAR. The design usually consists of medallions on a covered pink ground or occasionally on a very attractive red ground. Their shape is generally rather squarish, and because of their tight heavy weave they have a tendency to crack in shipment. They come in the more expensive price group.

Yahyah (Turkish), geometric carpets of very good wool and of good though not fine weave. They generally introduce medallions into the design and there is an overall blueish tinge to all the colours. They are the most attractive of contemporary Turkish production.

Yahyali, see YAHYAH

Yalmeh (Persian), from the Shiraz area. Factory made rugs, the production of which is only about twenty years old. Based loosely on Shiraz designs, made of good wool, thick but of coarse stitch and fairly loosely woven. Some have cotton warps and wefts which is rare for goods produced in the Shiraz region.

Yamout (Russian, Afghan, Persian), a Turkomen tribe producing some of the finest carpets of their type. The basic colour is very red or often a brownish-red shading to purple. The design usually introduces rows of diamond-shaped guls, and often incorporates a broad additional border at the ends. Some Yamout silk rugs and carpets are made in Persia.

Yarkand (Chinese), a carpet from Chinese Turkestan similar to SAMARKAND.

Yezd (Persian), town near Ispahan producing carpets similar in style to those of KIRMAN. The inhabitants, Zoroastrian in origin, have a reputation for producing reliable wares. This area also produces a type of cotton carpet, with simple designs and in bright colours, which is intended for domestic use and is seldom exported. Being knotted with cotton yarn, these carpets are not hard-wearing but they are useful for verandahs and outdoor use.

Yomut, see YAMOUT

Yuruk (Turkish), a nomadic type of rug made by KURDS in Caucasian types of design. They are sometimes called the poor man's KAZAK, but the fringes are so different that they cannot be confused with the real Kazaks. Their wool is good but softer than that of Kazaks (Plate 50).

Zarand (Persian), one of the many small areas near KIRMAN, producing similar carpets.

Appendix (ii) Glossary

This is a list of some of the more common technical terms used to describe oriental carpets. Many of them describe types of motifs or patterns; some describe sizes of carpets, or types of weave or knot. Some of the words are Persian; others have been coined by English-speaking dealers or collectors. All of them are useful when attempting to describe the appearance of an oriental carpet.

As with the list of Qualities, names printed in SMALL CAPITALS indicate that there is another entry in this glossary under that name.

AH, Anno Hegira, see DATES

Abradj, a change of colour at a certain place in a carpet, caused by a fresh supply of dyed wool being brought into use. This is a sign normally of small-scale homemade workmanship, though it is sometimes imitated on machine-made carpets (Plate 32)

Abrash, see ABRADJ

All-over, a term for a pattern that is repeated all over the FIELD of a carpet, without any MEDALLION or other central feature (Plates 5, 23 and 47)

Allah-Allah, an all-over design consisting of two inward-facing SERABEND patterns, with various motifs in between and surrounded by a frame (Plate 5)

Arabesque, an ornament in which interlacing TENDRILS are combined to form an eight-pointed MEDALLION

Ashkali, a motif used in the border of Kashkai carpets. It consists of a row of octagons with a line connecting them and lines in between them

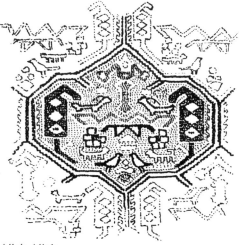

Allah-Allah

Arabesque

Audience Carpet, large carpets sometimes made with a plain matching ground for four pieces. They were arranged in a certain way for formal occasions

Baby, a rug measuring about 4ft × 2ft (1·20 × 0·60m)

112

Band, narrow strip of woven or knotted material for decorating tents, camel trappings, etc., especially among Turkomen tribes. See JOLAM

Barber's Pole, English name given to a pattern of oblique differently-coloured stripes in the border or medallion. It is common in Gendje

Bird Carpet, an antique type of Anatolian rug in which the design is based on a pattern of stylized leaf-forms resembling birds

Border, the band running round the edge of a carpet, enclosing the central FIELD. This always consists of a number of borders, of which one is wider, with narrower ones – called stripes or guards – on the outside and inside. The design of the border is usually complimentary to, but different from, that of the FIELD

Serabend border   Herati border

Boteh, a motif resembling a leaf, or a seed, with its tip bent sideways. In highly stylized forms it appears in the design of many oriental carpets (Plate 14). Variants are known as MIR and SERABEND, and it is the father of the Paisley design

Bottle Bag, see HOUDJIN

Camel Bag (or Juval), a piece resembling a small rug with a woven KILIM at one end as long as the rug itself. The sides were stitched together to form an open envelope, and they were hung in pairs over the back

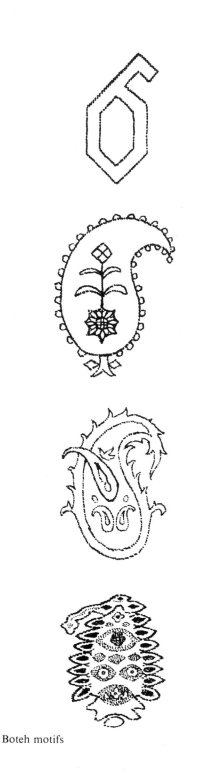

Boteh motifs

113

Boteh motifs

Cartouche designs

of a camel to carry the owner's possessions. Far rarer are bags where the piled part is only in narrow bands – it is then known as a JOLAM JUVAL (Plate 40)

Candlestick, see 'Y' MOTIF

Cartouche, an oval-shaped device, usually containing inscriptions or motifs. It sometimes appears on its own, sometimes pendant to a MEDALLION, and sometimes in a BORDER (Plates 11 and 18)

Chess Board, a design in which the FIELD is divided into a number of squares

Chintamani, a motif of three balls in a triangular arrangement. This was a Buddhist symbol and was probably introduced into Persian carpet design from China. Arranged in a pattern it is better known as the Badge of TAMERLANE

Chourouk, Turkish word meaning that the warp and weft of a carpet has rotted through getting wet and not drying out properly

Cloudband, a thin wavy pattern, probably introduced into Persian carpet design from China

Corner, a pattern decorating the four corners of the FIELD. Where this is introduced it is usually in conjunction with a central MEDALLION, and is frequently a quarter medallion

Covered Ground, a carpet with a MEDALLION and possibly CORNERS, whose GROUND is covered in small motifs (Plates 9, 16 and 17)

Crow's Foot, a typical motif in BORDERS

Cypress Tree, shown in silhouette, is common in Baktyar and at the sides of Mecca Shiraz prayer rugs and HAJI-HANUM Keshans (Plate 23)

Dates, AH is the date of Mohammed's flight from Mecca to Medina in AD 622 from which date Muslims tend to date their carpets. Western numerals can also be found in pieces made by Christians, mainly Armenians, who, of course, use the Gregorian calendar. Arabic numerals should be written from left to right, unlike Arabic writing which reads from right to left. It will be found, however, that these are sometimes written backwards or both ways (Plate 25) or even in mirror-writing. The date woven into a rug does not necessarily denote its age, it may merely mark some past event in the family of the weaver, see NUMBERS

114

Dog Tooth Border, an alternative name for MEDACHYL (See the inside side borders of Plate 13)

Dozar, the larger size of rug, measuring about 6ft 6in × 4ft 6in (2·00 × 1·40m).

Dragon Carpet, a motif seen in old Caucasian carpets, which is now believed to represent the skins of animals

Elephant's Foot, term for the octagon or GUL which constitutes the chief motif in many oriental carpets, especially Afghans (Plates 19 and 41).

Engsi, a rug intended to be hung over the entrance to a tent as a door flap. In Turkomen carpets these are usually decorated with a HATCHLI design (Plate 44)

Farsibaff, term for a Meshed carpet knotted with the Persian knots

Feraghan, an alternative name for the HERATI pattern

Field, the central area of a carpet enclosed by the BORDER

Figural, a carpet design introducing human figures. These are found more frequently in Kirman carpets than elsewhere (Plate 11)

Fringe, the WARP threads at the top and bottom of a carpet that hang loose, not being woven with the WEFT. Each pair, or sometimes four or more, is tied with a knot immediately adjoining the edge of the BORDER; a few inches of the thread then hang loose, or are sometimes partially tied together in a trellis design as in Plate 8

Garden Design, a carpet design popular especially in the eighteenth and early nineteenth centuries. It used to represent the layout of a Persian garden, with flowerbeds, paths, streams, and often birds and fishes, but is now very simple, generally from Baktyar, consisting of 'flower beds' divided by narrow bands (Plates 2 and 20)

Giordes, the Turkish knot, see KNOTS

Goblet Border, a characteristic motif in the border of Caucasian carpets. It is also called a wine glass border (Plate 46). The stylized goblets are usually placed between leaning serrated leaves, alternate ways up

Greek Key, a design often found in the narrow BORDERS of carpets. In a freely adapted form it is twisted into a hooked shape, when it is known as a RUNNING DOG pattern

Ground, an alternative name for the FIELD

Gul, a basic motif in the design of oriental carpets, especially Turkomen and Afghans. It is basically an octagon, but can be treated in many elaborate forms (Plates 19 and 41)

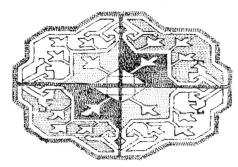

Yamout gul

Tekke gul

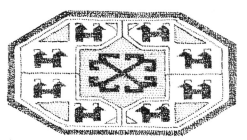

Yamout gul

115

Afghan gul

Pendik or Salor gul

Afghan gul

found in old Ispahans, Feraghans and Sines and in some modern goods

Hatchli, a carpet design incorporating a large cross on the entire FIELD, dividing it into four compartments. Both the arms of the cross and the quarters are usually highly decorated, and the two end 'borders' are not symmetrical (Plate 44)

Herati, a common pattern in Persian carpets. It consists of a central ROSETTE, surrounded by a diamond or LOZENGE, along the sides of which are four PALMETTES and from the sides of which hang four lanceolate leaves curving outwards. In a variant form this is also a popular BORDER pattern. This design is found in more qualities than any other and has been interpreted in a thousand different ways (Plate 4)

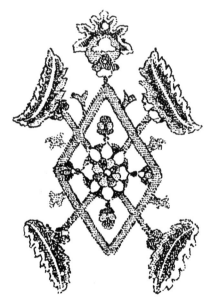

Haji-Hanum, a design generally of Keshan origin, usually with a central vase and flowers of prayer design, the whole being perhaps over-elaborate; the idea was to show the abundance, indeed the super abundance, of God's gifts to man (Plate 39)

Harshang, a motif reminiscent of a crab in shape

Hashti-Badomi, a rosette surrounded by eight BOTEHS in back-to-back pairs. It is

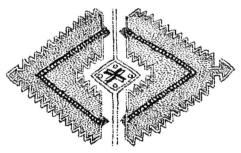

Herati designs

116

partly both. The term is also used for BOTTLE BAGS, which are used to carry leather bottles

Hourglass Border, geometric motif resembling two triangles touching at their apexes, like an egg-timer, with one dark and the other light in colour

Hunting Design, a carpet design popular in Persia especially in the sixteenth century. It depicted varieties of bird and game with huntsmen carrying bows and arrows or falcons, and sometimes mounted on horseback (Plate 13)

Jijim, a type of KILIM woven in four or five narrow BANDS not more than a foot wide, and then sewn together side by side

Jolam, a narrow strip from 6in to 2ft wide (15 to 60cm) and which may be up to 60ft (18m) or more long, used to decorate tents. Many decorative uses are being found for these in Western countries today

Herati designs

Herek, a small bedside rug, about 4ft × 2ft (1·20 × 0·60m)

Holbein Carpet, a type of Bergamo carpet as depicted in some paintings by Holbein

Houdjin, a small bag, usually half a SADDLE BAG, either all piled or all KILIM or

Karaja medallion designs

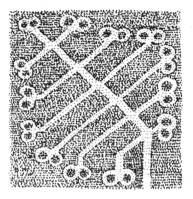

Karaja border design

Joshaghan, pattern based on an arrangement of diamond shapes, reminiscent of snow crystals. There may be a diamond MEDALLION in the centre of the FIELD, over which various stylized floral elements are grouped in diamond-shaped formations, as in Plate 16

Juval, a CAMEL BAG

Kachli, see HATCHLI

Karaja, a very distinctive geometric ground and border design from north-west Persia, usually with three medallions, two of which are similar, on a ground covered in small motifs

Kellegi, see KELLAY

Kellay, a piece between a carpet and a rug in size whose length is about double its width, though the name is given to most very long, very wide strips

Kenaré, the Persian name for a short STRIP

Kibitka, a small prayer niche found at the top of HATCHLI rugs, often in a row of five or six, as in Plate 44

Kilim, a woven carpet or rug without any knots, and therefore with no pile. They are normally reversible. Some knotted carpets have kilim borders at the top and bottom, notably the best of Herat Beloudj (Plates 32, 38 and 50)

Knots, (1) The *Giordes* or Turkish knot is made by looping the piece of yarn round two WARP threads and drawing it up between them, and is, therefore, sometimes called a closed knot. It is used in Turkey,

Turkish knot

Persian knot

Jufti knot

the Caucasus, parts of Persia and Afghanistan. In carpets made with this knot, the warp threads lie side by side and so when seen from the back show two bumps for each knot

(2) The *Sine* or Persian knot is also wound round two WARP threads, but only one end of the yarn is drawn up between them; the other one is drawn up outside on the left or on the right and this knot is sometimes known as an open knot. One warp will therefore tend to be pulled above

118

the other into the body of the carpet so that the back shows only one warp thread for each knot

(3) *Jufti* knots are a type of Sine knot which are woven over three or four warp threads. This makes for quicker weaving but a poorer quality as the resulting carpet will be less dense

Korani, a design imitating the gilt tooled bookbinding of the cover of the Koran. It is found particularly in Kirman carpets

Kufic Border, motif in, or resembling, the arabic kufic script

Lantern, or Hanging Lamp, a motif sometimes introduced, especially into PRAYER RUGS (Plate 48)

Latch Hooks, a common motif in many types of design

Leaf, a component of many designs.

Lanceolate leaves (spear-headed and curving outwards) occur in the HERATI pattern; serrated leaves, usually at an angle of 45° to the sides, occur around many BORDERS

Lozenge, an octagon. The term is normally applied to an oblong GUL-shaped design when used in BORDERS. See also CARTOUCHE

Maj-Nun, a stylized weeping willow. In older examples only half a tree was shown (Plate 23 and page 124)

Mat, a small rug of about 4 or 5 sq ft (0·4 to 0·5m²)

Meander, a line of motifs arranged to form a BORDER pattern. A succession of linked SWASTIKAS is found mainly in carpets from Chinese Turkestan

Medachyl, a crenellated or dogtooth BORDER (sometimes called a sugar-loaf border)

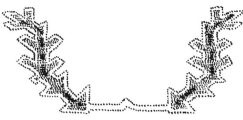

Leaf designs

Medallion design

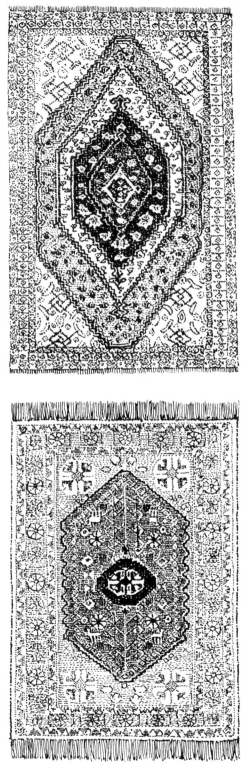

Medallions

Medallion designs

Medallion, the central motif in the FIELD of a carpet design. It may be geometric or floral; circular, square or rectangular; but is usually longer than it is wide, reflecting the proportions of the carpet. It may appear alone, or may be repeated and elements from its design may appear as CORNERS (Plates 7, 9, 16 and 28)

Mehrab, the niche in a PRAYER RUG. It comprises a pointed arch, often supported on pillars (Plates 26, 39, 42, 43 and 50).

Millefleurs, a design of small, symmetrically arranged, floral ornaments that was introduced into some oriental carpets, especially Kirmans, in the eighteenth century (Plates 30 and 39)

Mina Khani, a pattern consisting of a repetition of ROSETTES surrounded by petals in a LOZENGE-shaped formation. It is most usually found in Veramins and in Afghan Beshires in simplified form

Mir, a palm leaf leaning sideways, a common motif in Persian carpets. See also BOTEH

Miriboteh, a pattern consisting of the repetition of BOTEHS over the entire FIELD (Plates 14 and 38)

Mossul, a rug, mainly from the Hamadan district, measuring about 1 × 2m, but originally the name given to a quality

Nahni, a rectangular bag usually Kilim with four walls and a base similar to a child's carry-cot. Some say used as such, but more often seen on the backs of donkeys for the carriage and display of fruit

Naksha-i-Gashta, the general name given to new designs recently developed in Afghanistan

Namasé, a size of rug about 4ft × 2ft 6in (1·20 × 0·75m)

Namazlik, a prayer rug generally only applied to those of Afghan origin, eg Afghan BABIES and Herat Beloudj (Plate 42)

Numdah, a type of felt carpet made in India. They are decorative and extremely cheap but give very little wear

Numbers, Arabic numerals are as follows:

The top row is in the curvilinear style. The bottom row is in the kufic or rectilinear style. In both styles zero is represented by a dot. See also DATES

Open Ground, a carpet with a MEDALLION and possibly CORNERS, whose ground is of plain colour without designs (Plate 12)

Palmette, a large flower seen as if in section. This constitutes one of the most common motifs in the decoration of Persian carpets.

Pendjerelik, a type of rug intended to be hung over the entrance to a tent. Its purpose is similar to the ENGSI, but its shape is

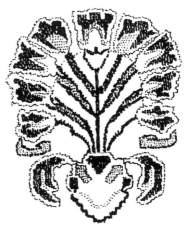

Palmette designs

quite different, being as long as a small rug but only up to 18in (45cm) deep. A long woollen fringe, up to 4ft (1·20m) in length, is woven down its length with the object of letting in some light but keeping out heat and flies

Persian Knots, see KNOTS

Penj-Renk Persian for five (Penj) colour (Renk), used to describe modern carpets, mainly Keshan, woven in only five or six colours, usually beiges or soft blues on a cream ground and almost never with red. They tend to have a washed-out look and become dirty easily

Piece, the general term for a rug or carpet of any kind

Pine Cone, an alternative term for the MIRIBOTEH pattern

Polonaise, an inaccurate term for a type of Persian carpet made in the seventeenth century, probably in Keshan, and used largely as presentation pieces to foreign monarchs. It was normally woven with silk and metal thread

Pomegranate, a common motif in Samarkand carpets

Prayer Rug, a rug, whose design contains a MEHRAB at one end. (See pages 123 and 124)

Prophet's Green, a dark green with a tinge of orange

Pushti, a Persian term for a MAT

Quality, a trade term for a distinct type of rug or carpet, as made in a certain district. Thus, you may have a good quality or a poor quality rug of a certain quality (type)

Ram's Horn, a pattern sometimes found on Shirvan rugs, and Turkomen prayer rugs (Plates 42 and 43 and page 123)

Riz, a unit of measurement for Tabriz carpets

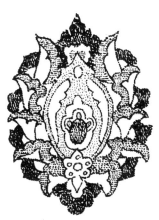

Palmette designs

Prayer rugs

Rosette, a flower seen as if full-face. A number of petals arranged symmetrically round a central calyx. This is a common motif in the design of carpets

Running Dog, a design for carpet BORDERS, developed from the GREEK KEY

'S' Border, a characteristic motif in the BORDER of old Caucasian carpets

Saddle Bag, two small bags, similar to a CAMEL BAG but made in one piece, intended to be hung over the neck of a horse or donkey, and hence double-ended

Saddle Cloth, a rug, piled or of kilim, for hanging over the back of a horse or donkey saddle (Plate 37)

Safavid, the dynasty ruling Persia from the sixteenth to the eighteenth centuries which

123

Ram's Horn design

Prayer rugs

Rosette designs

124

Rosette designs

saw the Persian Renaissance under SHAH ABBAS

Saff, a type of PRAYER RUG. See Qualities of Carpets

Sedjadé, a size of rug about 6ft 6in × 4ft 3in (2·00 × 1·30m)

Senneh Knot, see SINE KNOT

Serabend, a pattern of small palm leaves, otherwise MIR, tilted sideways (Plates 1, 14 and 38)

Shah Abbas, a design based on the repetition of large PALMETTES and ROSETTES over the FIELD, linked by branches or tendrils, normally as an ALL-OVER design. It is reputed to be the design most favoured by Shah Abbas

Sile, see ZILLE

Sine, a variant of the HERATI pattern

Sine Knot, the Persian knot, see KNOTS

Skirt, an additional BORDER usually at each end, differing from all the others, often found in Turkomen carpets and rugs (Plates 24 and 44)

Soumak, a type of woven carpet similar to the KILIM in that there is no pile (Plate 35). It differs, however, in that the weft threads composing the pattern are left hanging loose for several inches on the back of the rug, which thus acquires a quite distinctive appearance similar to a shaggy fleece. This gives them greater warmth than a kilim, but an underfelt is very necessary to enable them to lie flat on the floor (see Qualities of Carpets)

Strip, a long narrow piece of carpet for corridors or stairs

Sutural Border, a border composed of zig-zag lines forming adjacent triangles

Swastika, the crooked cross motif, of ancient Chinese origin, and originally considered a symbol of good luck. It sometimes appears on carpets, especially as the MEANDER pattern

'T' Border, a common pattern in carpets from Chinese Turkestan

Tabachi, wool from the backs of dead sheep. This is far inferior in quality to wool sheared from live animals but is sometimes used for the manufacture of cheap carpets

Tamerlane, or Badge of Tamerlane, a pattern composed of rows of CHINTAMANI

Tarantula, a motif resembling a stylized spider often woven into Turkomen rugs

Tendril, the sinuous stem of a plant. These are introduced into many carpet designs: they frequently appear in narrow BORDERS, and constitute an important element in the HERATI and ARABESQUE patterns

Transylvanian Rugs, an inaccurate name for a type of antique Anatolian rug of which specimens have been found in Hungarian Protestant churches

Tree of Life, a stylized representation of a tree, with a trunk and branches. This can be found in both geometric and pictorial form (Plate 26)

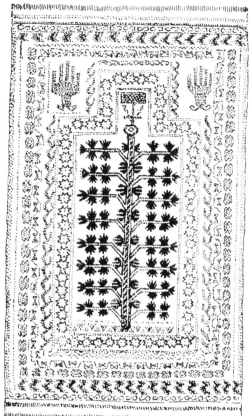

Tree of Life designs

Tree of Life, Weeping Willow form

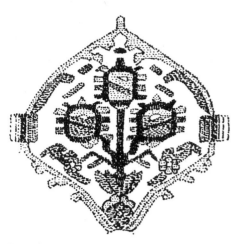

Vase design

Turkbaff, term for a Meshed carpet knotted with Turkish knots, and of better quality

Vase, a motif used in the ZILLI-SULTAN design (Plates 29 and 39)

Warp, the threads running from top to bottom of any woven material

Weft, the threads running from side to side of any woven material

Wine Glass, see GOBLET BORDER

'X' Hook, a typical motif in nomad rugs

'Y' Motif, a stylized geometric shape, resembling a double candlestick, common in the design of Turkomen rugs

Yastik, the Turkish name for a very small rug, often smaller than a MAT and originally intended as a prayer hassock. Often less than 1ft × 1ft (30 × 30cm), they are used today as handbags by trendy youngsters

Zar, a unit of area about 13½ to 16½sq ft (1·20 to 1·50m²). The area varies from district to district: from about 13½ to 14½sq ft (1·20 to 1·30m²) in Hamadan up to about 15½ to 16½sq ft (1·40 to 1·50m²) in Shiraz

Zaronim, a size of rug, about 20sq ft (1·80m²) being a ZAR and a half – NIM is Persian for half

Zille, a KILIM, generally of Russian origin, and of similar weave to a SOUMAK. It is generally found in a carpet size of about 10ft × 5ft (3·00 × 1·50m), and is often made in two narrow bands which are then sewn together. The design was originally a stylized dragon but this has now become so over-simplified that it merely looks like a large S or Z

Zilli-Sultan, an all-over pattern using a vase of flowers as its motif, often with a bird on each side. Some authorities, however, apply this name to a design consisting of the repetition of small stylized flower motifs

Vase designs

127

Appendix (iii) Further Study

Museums

London Victoria and Albert Museum
Notably, the Ardebil carpet, a superb example of the Persian classic period, made for the Ardebil mosque in AD 1539, probably in Tabriz. Also the Chelsea carpet, Persian sixteenth-century, of similar date and design to the Ardebil carpet; and a fine large Vase carpet, probably Kirman, that once belonged to William Morris

Cambridge, England Fitzwilliam Museum
Exhibits can be touched, properly examined and walked upon!

Paris Musée des Arts Décoratifs

Lyons Musée Historique des Tissus
Unquestionably the best collection of its kind in the world, illustrating the history of cloth weaving from the earliest times and in all its forms

Vienna Osterreichisches Museum für Angewandte Kunst
An important collection, including a fine Hunting carpet, entirely of silk and embroidered with silver and silver-gilt thread, made in Keshan about 1550

Milan Poldi Pezzoli Museum
Notably a superb Hunting carpet made in Keshan, probable date 1543

Stockholm Statens Historika Museum
Notably the Marby rug, an early Caucasian rug probably dating from the first half of the fifteenth century

Berlin Staatliche Museen
Including many early pieces acquired by the outstanding scholar, Wilhelm von Bode

New York Metropolitan Museum
Extremely important and early pieces from the collections of Joseph V. McMullan and John D. Rockefeller Jr. An exceptional 360-page catalogue has recently been published

Washington DC Textile Museum Collection

Cambridge, Mass Fogg Art Museum

Boston Museum of Fine Arts

Philadelphia Museum of Art

Los Angeles County Museum
Notably the smaller companion piece to the Ardebil carpet

Books

Edwards, A. Cecil, *The Persian Carpet*, 1953

Erdmann, Kurt, *Oriental Carpets: an account of their history*, 1962

Fokker, Nicolas, *Persian and other Oriental Carpets for Today*, 1973

Ford, P. R. J., *Oriental Carpet Designs*, 1981

Gans-Reudin, E., *Modern Oriental Carpets*, 1971

Hubel, Reinhard G., *The Book of Carpets*, 1970

Jacobsen, Charles W., *Check Points on How to Buy Oriental Rugs*, 1969

Jacoby, Heinrich, *How to know Oriental Carpets and Rugs*, 1962

Landreau, Anthony N. and Pickering, W. R., *From the Bosphorus to Samarkand: Flat-Woven Rugs*, 1969

Larson, Knut, *Rugs and Carpets of the Orient*, 1966

Liebetrau, Preben, *Oriental Rugs in Colour*, 1962

Neff, Ivan C. and Mages, Carol V., *Dictionary of Oriental Carpets*, 1977

Schürmann, Ulrich, *Central Asian Rugs*, 1969; and any of this author's other books

von Bode, Wilhelm and Kühnel, Ernst, *Antique Rugs from the Near East*, 4th edition 1970